...I am not ashamed of the Gospel. It is the power of God for the salvation of everyone who believes...

—*Romans 1:16*

...immediately they left their boat and their father and followed him.

—*Matthew 4:22*

God does not deign to save His people by means of dialectics: the kingdom of God is in the simplicity of faith, not in contentious words.

—*St. Ambrose of Milan*

"I first learned about Greg's wonderful booklet when I was monitoring the CHN email list and one of our regulars mentioned it as a great apologetics tool. After getting a copy, I had to agree—it backs up Catholic doctrine with loads of Scripture and understandable commentary, just right for the inquisitive Christian. With Greg's generosity, CHN began sending them to those looking into the Church. Great for RCIA, Bible study, Confirmation, and spreading the truth about the Catholic Church."

-Chris LaRose
Former Assistant Director, Coming Home Network

Having come from a Bible-only background, I found Catholic Doctrine in Scripture helpful as a ready reference to find the scriptures that demonstrated Catholic teaching. The Bible is truly a Catholic book and as Catholics we need to be able to defend our faith from sacred scripture. Now, as a RCIA and Small Christian Community leader, I have given a number of copies to those preparing to enter the Church. I greatly appreciate Greg's work in gathering these scriptures into one place.

-Patty Bonds
Catholic convert and author

"Only God really knows how many lives this book has touched. It has been a welcome answer to the questions so often asked by Fundamentalists and Evangelicals: Where does it say that in the Bible? As a former Protestant, I know all too well how that game is played. Catholics do not memorize chapter and verse as Protestants do, and they are accused of not knowing the Bible. This is a specious argument, but it works with Catholics who don't know their faith well. This book is a welcome, much needed antidote."

-Jay Damien
Catholic convert and apologist

"After reading *Catholic Doctrine in Scripture* I was convinced that the Catholic Church has a very strong Scriptural basis for her teaching and that there are many Protestant teachings that do not take into account some of the verses that Catholic theology includes. I know now that the Catholic Church is the true Church and the one Christ Himself founded. I found the book to be just the thing to get me over the hurdles I had."

- April LaCoursiere
Catholic convert

"My bother-in-law was thrilled to have the book. He said that his kids were beginning to get older and they asked him questions about the Catholic Faith that he didn't know how to answer. He said *Catholic Doctrine in Scripture* gave him the ability to respond."

- Jackie Zimmerer
Catholic convert and author

Gregory Oatis' book, *Catholic Doctrine in Scripture*, is a highly useful, delightful tool for Catholics and other Christians to learn more about the profound biblical grounding of the Catholic faith. I am especially impressed by its comprehensiveness: no less than 53 topics are dealt with. The impact of the sheer accumulation of biblical indications for distinctively Catholic doctrines is overwhelming and cannot fail to have an effect on any reader, whether they agree with the author's conclusions or not. Holy Scripture is not the exclusive domain of our esteemed Protestant brethren. We rejoice in their admirable love for God's Revelation (and can learn much from it), but it is time that we started "reclaiming" the Bible for the purposes of a confident Catholic apologetic and the strengthening of faith. Catholics have had an "inferiority complex" in this regard for far too long. I heartily recommend this work for Catholics and non-Catholics alike.

–Dave Armstrong
Catholic convert and author of 'A Biblical Defense of Catholicism' and 'More Biblical Evidence for Catholicism'

CATHOLIC DOCTRINE
IN
SCRIPTURE

CATHOLIC DOCTRINE
IN
SCRIPTURE

BY GREGORY OATIS
CHResources

Coming Home Resources
P.O. Box 8290
Zanesville, Ohio 43702

Coming Home Resources is a registered trademark
of the Coming Home Network International, Inc.

ISBN 0-9702621-4-0

Cover design by Devin Schadt, Saint Louis Creative.
Layoutt and design using Pagemaker 7.0 by Shala Hennessy.

CONTENTS

FOREWORD

There are not over a hundred people in the United States who hate the Catholic Church. There are millions, however, who hate what they wrongly believe to be the Catholic Church—which is, of course, quite a different thing. These millions can hardly be blamed for hating Catholics because Catholics "adore statues;" because they "put the Blessed Mother on the same level with God;" because they "say indulgence is a permission to commit sin;" because the Pope "is a Fascist;" because the Church "is the defender of Capitalism." If the Church taught or believed any one of these things, it should be hated, but the fact is that the Church does not believe nor teach any one of them. It follows then that the hatred of the millions is directed against error and not against truth. As a matter of fact, if we Catholics believed all of the untruths and lies which were said against the Church, we probably would hate the Church a thousand times more than they do.

If I were not a Catholic, and were looking for the true Church in the world today, I would look for the one Church which did not get along well with the world; in other words, I would look for the Church which the world hates. My reason for doing this would be, that if Christ is in any one of the churches of the world today, He must still be hated as He was when He was on earth in the flesh. If you would find Christ today, then find the Church that does not get along with the world. Look for the Church that is hated by the world, as Christ was hated by the world. Look for the Church which is accused of being behind the times, as Our Lord was accused of being ignorant and never having learned. Look for the Church which men sneer at as socially inferior, as they sneered at Our Lord because He came from Nazareth. Look for the Church which is accused of having a devil, as Our Lord was accused of being possessed by Beelzebub, the Prince of Devils. Look for the Church which the world rejects because it claims it is infallible, as Pilate rejected Christ because he called Himself the Truth. Look for the Church which amid the confusion of conflicting opinions, its members love as they love Christ, and respect its voice as the very voice of its Founder, and the suspicion will grow, that if the Church is unpopular with the spirit of the world, then it is unworldly, and if it is unworldly, it is other-worldly. Since it is other-worldly, it is infinitely loved and infinitely hated as was Christ Himself. ... the Catholic Church is the only Church existing today which goes back to the time of Christ. History is so very clear on this point, it is curious how many miss its obviousness...

(By: Bishop Fulton Sheen, ©1938 by Radio Replies Press Society, St. Paul, Minnesota ©1979 by TAN Books and Publishers, Inc., Rockford, Illinois. Used by permission.)

PREFACE

This book was compiled by a Catholic layman, to allow thinking, seeking, Bible-loving Christians to evaluate for themselves the scriptural basis for Catholic teaching. My premise is simple: Only one Church was there to walk the stony shores of Galilee with Jesus; only one did He found upon Peter, the Rock, whom He directed to feed His lambs; only one received from Him the keys to the Kingdom of God and, with them, the power to bind and loose on earth and in heaven; only one was sitting at His feet as He explained His parables; only one was there to witness the water turning to wine, the feeding of the five thousand, the healing of the ten lepers, and the raising of Lazarus; only one was with Him as He staggered up the face of a hill named Golgotha; and only one was there three days later to see the stone rolled aside and the wrappings dropped in a pile in the corner of the tomb; only one received the Holy Spirit like fire in a closed room on Pentecost; only one was proclaimed by Peter and James through the narrow streets of Jerusalem; only one was preached tirelessly by Paul through the cities of the ancient empire, even to the capital, Rome itself. All of this means that if you believe the Catholic Church to be a misguided, deceitful, unbiblical cult, you must say the same about the apostles and their successors, the ones who after receiving the Catholic faith, carefully and lovingly passed it on to succeeding generations—often, at the cost of their lives. The unmistakable truth of the matter is this: The religion that is revealed in the Bible, in both the Old and the New Testaments, is utterly and wholly, totally, unequivocally and gloriously Catholic. Over the past 2,000 years there have been 265 popes, dating back to Peter himself. Each one has exercised the same authority given by Jesus to Peter alone among the apostles, to tend His flock (Jn. 21:15-17). In sum, it is the Catholic Church that is the only true Bible Church. Her history and her teachings are outlined in every page of the sacred scriptures.

Are you skeptical? Wonderful! Because you are holding the evidence in your hands. Weigh it for yourself. And prove me wrong if you're able.

This project was begun as a private reference tool for use in discussion settings, since surprisingly few Catholics—and, more understandably, even fewer Protestants—are aware of the scripture verses which affirm the most basic tenets of the Catholic faith, including the Real Presence of Jesus in the Holy Eucharist, the authority of the Church, the requirements for salvation, St. Peter as the first pope, devotion to Mary, infant Baptism and free will. And so this book focuses on the passages that establish those key doctrines. It also touches on other, less central issues which have nonetheless been traditional points of debate between Protestants and Catholics – including "graven images," calling priests "father," purgatory, mortal and venial sins, the veneration of relics, and even guardian angels.

Because this book is intended only as a guide, I urge you to consult your Bible as you review these passages, so you will be able to examine the contexts in their entirety. We so often see verses torn from the page and used to support claims that are contrary to both the letter and the spirit of the Word. Indeed, if one were simply to read the contexts from which they were wrenched, most of these misconceptions would be easily resolved. It's entirely possible that not all of the notes and references found here will be instantly clear and comprehensible to every individual. After all, this project evolved from personal notes. But don't be deterred; I am certain most interested Christians will be able to sift through the greater part without much difficulty. It is, after all, important to consider carefully the truth of what we hear – and not to simply accept the "traditions of men." For, as St. Peter himself warns us: "...there will be false teachers among you, who will introduce destructive heresies and even deny the Master who ransomed them, bringing swift destruction on themselves. Many will follow their licentious ways..." St. Paul adds: "Let no one deceive you in any way."

-G.O.

CHURCH AUTHORITY AND PAPAL INFALLIBILITY

Lk. 10:16 – "Whoever listens to you listens to me. Whoever rejects you rejects me. And whoever rejects me rejects the one who sent me." Jesus himself says it clearly and without equivocation: The Church speaks for Christ.

1 Tim. 3:15 – St. Paul calls the Church—and not the scriptures—the foundation of truth: "But if I should be delayed, you should know how to behave in the household of God, which is the church of the living God, the pillar and foundation of truth."

Rom. 13:1-2 – "Let every person be subordinate to the higher authorities, for there is no authority except from God, and those that exist have been established by God. Therefore, whoever resists authority opposes what God has appointed, and those who oppose it will bring judgment upon themselves." God has ordained that his community of faith be hierarchical, not democratic. And we see all of the major faith traditions of mankind likewise recognizing the spiritual value of a soul submitting to an authority greater than itself.

Heb. 13:17 – "Obey your leaders and defer to them, for they keep watch over you..." The Church hierarchy is ordained by God. The Bible tells us we are obliged to follow the leadership of the Church.

Mt. 28:18-20 – "All power in heaven and on earth has been given to me. Go, therefore, and make disciples of all nations, baptizing them in the name of the Father, and of the Son, and of the holy Spirit, teaching them to observe all I have commanded you. And behold, I am with you always, until the end of the age." Jesus' authority is passed on to his Church, and it will never fail.

Eph. 3:10 – Even the angels are instructed by the Church: "...so that the manifold wisdom of God might now be made known through the church to the principalities and authorities in the heavens." This is an astonishing statement. And note that St. Paul does *not* say here—or anywhere else— that the angels are instructed by the scriptures, although he certainly could have.

Jn. 11:47-52 – St. John states clearly that even Caiaphas was inspired by the Holy Spirit when, speaking from the chair of Moses, he declared that Jesus must die so the whole nation might not perish: "He (Caiaphas) did not say this on his own, but since he was high priest for that year, he prophesied..." If, as the scriptures tell us, the Holy Spirit spoke through the unchristian conniver Caiaphas, how is it He cannot speak through a faithful and learned Christian pope?

14

Mt. 23:1-3 – Jesus acknowledges the authority of even the Pharisees when they teach from the chair of Moses. Note that the scriptures specifically include the disciples in the directive to obey the Pharisees. Jesus clearly feels that obedience to ordained spiritual authority is important: "Then Jesus spoke to the crowds and to his disciples, saying, 'The scribes and the Pharisees have taken their seat on the chair of Moses. Therefore, do and observe all things whatsoever they tell you, but do not follow their example.'" Also, be aware that Jesus' command is quite sweeping in its scope. He says his followers should "do and observe all things whatsoever" which their rightful spiritual leaders direct. Jesus does not leave us much leeway to exclude items we might perceive as difficult or burdensome.

1 Jn. 4:6 – "We belong to God, and anyone who knows God listens to us, while anyone who does not belong to God refuses to hear us. This is how we know the spirit of truth and the spirit of deceit." Submission to apostolic authority is the hallmark of faithfulness.

Eph. 2:19-20 – The Church stands upon the solid rock of salvation history. According to St. Paul, it is the "...household of God, built upon the foundation of the apostles and the prophets, with Christ Jesus himself as the capstone."

Mt. 18:15-18 – The Bible tells us to take our disagreements to the Church, not to the scriptures: "If he refuses to listen even to the church, then treat him as you would a Gentile or a tax collector." This command parallels the following passage:

Deut. 17:8-12 – The Old Testament contains its own form of the Magisterium—the teaching authority of the Church. It is clear here that disagreements were to be settled by priests and judges, not by dueling interpretations: "Any man who has the insolence to refuse to listen to the priest who officiates there in the ministry of the Lord, your God, or to the judge, shall die." Nowhere—in the Old Testament or the New—are the scriptures cited as the supreme authority of faith.

Eph. 3:4-6 – "When you read this you can understand my insight into the mystery of Christ, which was not made known to human beings in other generations as it has now been revealed to his holy apostles and prophets by the Spirit..." Revelation comes to us through the Church. There is no reason whatsoever to suppose that every individual will receive direct, personal and spontaneous inspiration from the Holy Spirit.

Acts 15:30-31 – Paul and Barnabas take the Church's teachings—its dogmas—to Antioch: "Upon their arrival in Antioch they called the assembly together and delivered the letter." Apparently the apostles did not trust the individual communities' ability to discern the truth using "scripture alone." They circulated letters, which carried the weight of apostolic authority, just as the Church does today.

Acts 16:4 – Paul and Timothy take Church dogmas to world: "As they traveled from city to city, they handed to the people for observance the decisions reached by the apostles and presbyters in Jerusalem." The apostles expected that their mandates would be obeyed because of the authority given to them by God, not because of any especially eloquent appeals they made to the "scripture alone." In other words, they had authority that existed apart from the scriptures, even though all of what they taught coincided with the truths of scripture. The same is true of the Church today.

Eph. 5:25-27 – "...Even as Christ loved the church and handed himself over for her to sanctify her... that he might present to himself the church in splendor, without spot or wrinkle... that she might be holy and without blemish." At first glance, this seems a surprising statement—that Jesus was crucified to sanctify the Church. But upon reflection we see that it must be so, for the Church is his own Mystical Body (1 Cor. 12:12-27), and it is through him—and therefore through his Church—that salvation comes.

Num. 12:1-15 – Miriam, Moses' sister, rebels, along with Aaron. She says: "Is it through Moses alone that the Lord speaks? Does he not speak through us also?" Miriam is rendered leprous for her refusal to submit to God's anointed authority. Hers is the same objection we hear from so many Protestant brethren who balk at the hierarchical structure of the Mystical Body. Yet the family of God has always been a hierarchy—never a democracy.

Num. 16:1-35 – Korah objects to the authority of the hierarchy: "They stood before Moses and held an assembly against Moses and Aaron, to whom they said, 'Enough from you! The whole community, all of them, are holy; the Lord is in their midst. Why then should you set yourselves over the Lord's congregation?' ...They went down alive to the nether world with all belonging to them; the earth closed over them, and they perished from the community..." Again we see clearly that the community of the faithful is hierarchical, and those who refuse to submit to it are punished. It is interesting to note that many people today who object to "organized religion" make much the same argument

Jude 4-11 – The revolt of Korah is referred to: "They followed the way of Cain... and perished in the rebellion of Korah." (See passage immediately above.) Jude is here referring to persons within the early Christian community who were resisting the authority of the apostles and urging the new Christians to return to the Mosaic law. Clearly, the authority of God does not reside with each individual, but rather it lies with the anointed leaders who have been ordained by the power of God through the authority vested in the apostles by Christ Jesus himself.

Num. 11:27-29 – "…When a young man quickly told Moses, 'Eldad and Medad are prophesying in the camp,' Joshua, son of Nun, who from his youth had been Moses' aide, said, 'Moses, my lord, stop them.' But Moses answered him, 'Are you jealous for my sake? Would that all the people of the Lord were prophets! Would that the Lord might bestow his spirit on them all!'" So we see that the Holy Spirit is not automatically poured out upon all the faithful—and this is the basis for the false doctrine of "sola scriptura," that the Holy Spirit will automatically lead all the faithful to the truth of the scriptures, or, in other words, that he will turn all into prophets. This has never been the case, regardless of what Moses may have wished.

Jn. 14:16-18 – "…I will ask the Father, and he will give you another Advocate to be with you always." Jesus' promise of infallibility is implicit in the word "always." We know that Jesus is speaking here to his apostles since this passage is part of his Last Supper discourse.

Jn. 14:25 – "…The Holy Spirit that the Father will send in my name—he will teach you everything and remind you of all that I told you." Again, Jesus' promise of infallibility is clear in his use of the collectives, "everything" and "all." He does not equivocate. Note that here he is again talking to his apostles.

Jn. 16:13 – "…When he comes, the Spirit of truth, he will guide you to all truth." Jesus' promise to the Church he instituted is immense and sweeping. And the fact that the Church has remained doctrinally consistent for two thousand years—often in the face of severe pressure from secular authorities and trends of popular thought—is proof that Jesus has kept his promise.

1 Pet. 5:2-3 – "Tend the flock of God in your midst… Do not lord it over those assigned to you, but be examples to the flock." Peter is speaking with great authority here. If he were not in a special leadership role, he would not be able to command others to lead.

2 Pet. 1:20 – "Know this first of all, that there is no prophecy of scripture that is a matter of personal interpretation…" The scriptures are clearly beneficial for our instruction, but our own personal interpretations are not to be considered authoritative. Note the importance which St. Peter attaches to this truth: "Know this first of all…"

2 Pet. 2:1-2 – "…There will be false teachers among you, who will introduce destructive heresies and even deny the Master who ransomed them, bringing swift destruction on themselves. Many will follow their licentious ways…" This passage is often used to defend belief in the supposed "Great Apostasy," which claims that the entire Catholic Church vaulted into error immediately after Jesus' death. But the passage actually proves the contrary point, that the entire Church cannot possibly have apostatized, or there would not have remained a "you" for the "false teachers" to be "among."

2 Pet. 3:16 – "…There are some things hard to understand that the ignorant and unstable distort to their own destruction, just as they do the other scriptures." The scriptures cannot be our supreme authority. There will always be the question of interpretation. Without an authoritative voice to interpret them—a voice that's guided by the Holy Spirit—discord will reign. This is what we see in the tens of thousands of Protestant denominations that exist in America today. While they all agree that the scriptures are their ultimate authority, no two denominations can agree on what the scriptures are actually saying.

1 Thess. 5:12-13 – "We ask you, brothers, to respect those who are laboring among you and who are over you in the Lord and who admonish you, and to show esteem for them with special love on account of their work." As always, St. Paul upholds the hierarchy of the Church.

1 Cor. 14:37-38 – Church authority takes precedence over personal discernment: "If anyone thinks that he is a prophet or a spiritual person, he should recognize that what I am writing to you is a commandment of the Lord. If anyone does not acknowledge this, he is not acknowledged."

Eph. 4:11-16 – "And he gave some as apostles, others as prophets, others as evangelists, others as pastors and teachers, to equip the holy ones for the work of ministry, for building up the body of Christ, until we all attain to the unity of faith and knowledge of the Son of God…so that we may no longer be infants, tossed by waves and swept along by every wind of teaching arising from human trickery…" The Bible says the Church is our protection against apostasy.

Gal. 1:8 – "But even if we or an angel from heaven should preach [to you] a gospel other than the one that we preached to you, let that one be accursed. As we have said before, and now I say again, if anyone preaches to you a gospel other than the one that you received, let that one be accursed!" We should not believe interpretations of the Word that are not endorsed by the apostolic authority of the Church. The scriptures are not meant to operate like a Rorschach test, with each individual filling in his or her own meaning.

Lk. 11:17 – "Every kingdom divided against itself will be laid waste, and house will fall against house." Since the Reformation, Christianity has been continually divided, subdivided and subdivided again. Clearly, this is not God's plan. The Church established by Christ was in no way intended to be "denominational," but rather "catholic"—i.e., unified and universal. For further evidence of this, see Jesus' beautiful and inspiring unity prayer in John 17:20-23.

Eph. 1:22-23 – "And he put all things beneath his feet and gave him as head over all things to the church, which is his body, the fullness of the one who fills all things in every way." St. Paul teaches that the Church is the Mystical Body of Christ. It makes no more sense for Christianity to be divided than it would for a body to be divided.

PETER AS THE FIRST POPE

Peter is clearly depicted as the first among the apostles, both by Jesus and by the evangelists. Peter is mentioned 191 times in the New Testament. All the other apostles combined are mentioned by name just 130 times. And the most commonly referenced apostle apart from Peter is John, whose name appears 48 times. Peter's authority is unquestioned, even by Paul. And Peter's name appears first in virtually every listing of the apostles, just as Judas' name always appears last. If there is a reason for the latter—which there obviously is—on what basis can we deny there is a reason for the former?

Mt. 16:15-19 – "Blessed are you, Simon, son of Jonah...you are Peter, and upon this rock I will build my church, and the gates of the netherworld shall not prevail against it. I will give you the keys to the kingdom of heaven. Whatever you bind on earth will be bound in heaven; and whatever you loose on earth shall be loosed in heaven." Some Protestant apologists make much of the fact that the two words for "rock" in the original Greek text, *petros* and *petra*, have different gender endings. They claim that the gender ending results in different meanings—usually, in the size of the "rock" in question. But the different gender endings are simply due to the fact that a man's name cannot have a feminine ending, while the Greek word for "rock" does. The error in the Protestant position becomes abundantly clear when one realizes that in the Aramaic language, which Jesus spoke, there were no gender endings for nouns. So when Jesus spoke this sentence, he would have been saying, "...you are rock, and upon this rock I will build my church. ..." There would have been no difference whatsoever in the endings of the words; it would have been the exact same word used twice. This is just one example of Protestant believers reading the scriptures through the lens of their traditions, and missing the clear and obvious sense of certain key passages. The fact is, these are profoundly important verses, for they contain Jesus' unequivocal promise to protect and guide the Church he is to found, through St. Peter, to whom he entrusts the keys to the kingdom (see next item). Whenever God renames someone, he is calling our attention to a truly momentous event—as in Abram to Abraham, Jacob to Israel, Saul to Paul and Simon to Rock.

Is. 22:15-25 – Eliakim is given the keys of the kingdom, thus becoming the most powerful man in the realm apart from the king himself. The keys are the sign of the royal authority. Because the keys are passed on to each successive officeholder, they indicate that the office lives on even after the individual who holds it dies. The king does not stop appointing stewards when one dies—the keys are passed along to another. Thus, Jesus' royal authority did not die with Peter but was passed on to the next generation, as it will be until the end of time.

1 Cor. 15:3-5 – According to St. Paul, St. Peter was singled out by Jesus after the resurrection: "For I handed on to you as of first importance what I also received: that Christ died for our sins in accordance with the scriptures; that he was buried; that he was raised on the third day in accordance with the scriptures; that he appeared to Cephas, then to the Twelve." Note too that St. Paul refers to St. Peter by the name Jesus gave him: *Cephas*, which is, "Rock." This reference by Paul is alone enough to refute the alternative interpretations given for Mt. 16:15-19 (see above). For example, if the word "Rock" referred not to Peter, but to Peter's faith, then St. Paul would be making a terrible blunder in referring to Simon himself as "Rock." No, in the passage from Matthew, Jesus himself was clearly giving Simon a new name, "Rock," indicating a change in his status that was to have a momentous impact on salvation history.

Rev. 3:7 – "The holy one, the true, who holds the key of David, who opens and no one shall close, who closes and no one shall open, says this..." The keys belong to Jesus. In scripture, they are the sign of his authority. When he gives the keys to St. Peter in Matthew 16, he is simply delegating the authority, which is his for all eternity. Thus, as

Eliakim before him (see Is. 22:15-25), St. Peter is chief steward of the kingdom who wields the king's authority.

Gal. 1:18 – After St. Paul receives his revelations from the Holy Spirit, he travels to Jerusalem specifically to confer with St. Peter: "Then after three years I went up to Jerusalem to confer with Cephas..." This is an awesome indication of the position of authority, which St. Peter occupied. Also note that once again Paul refers to Peter by the name Jesus gave him—*Cephas*, or "Rock."

Is. 51:1-2 – "Look to the rock from which you were hewn, to the pit from which you were quarried; Look to Abraham, your father, and to Sarah, who gave you birth..." Abraham was the patriarch of the old covenant, and his name was changed by God to underscore his status. Abraham was also, in the passage quoted here, the only man referred to as "rock" until Jesus referred to Peter that way. Elsewhere, that metaphor was reserved for God (Deut. 32:4; 1 Sam. 2:2; Ps. 18:3, etc.). So not only by referring to Simon as "Rock," but also by changing his name in the process, Jesus is establishing an undeniable parallel between Simon Peter and Abraham. Peter is the patriarch of the new covenant, just as Abraham was the patriarch of the old.

Acts 2:14-36 – "Then Peter stood up with the Eleven, raised his voice, and proclaimed..." This is the first Christian sermon detailed in scripture. Already St. Peter's status as leader is clear, as shown by the title, "the Eleven," which never included Peter.

Lk. 22:31-32 – Jesus prays for St. Peter alone among the apostles: "Simon, Simon, behold Satan has demanded to sift all of you like wheat, but I have prayed that your own faith may not fail; and once you have turned back, you must strengthen your brothers." Peter receives special attention from Jesus. Jesus observes that Satan is seeking to break the apostles' faith. Jesus' response is to pray for Peter and to direct him to hold the rest of the apostles firm. Jesus' statement dovetails perfectly with Peter's role as the "Rock" upon which the Church rests, and with the pope's role in Church history.

Acts 15 – St. Paul and St. Barnabas struggle with the claims of the Judaisers. They travel to Jerusalem where Peter and the apostles set about addressing the matter of whether a Christian must follow Mosaic law and be circumcised: "...it was decided that Paul, Barnabas, and some of the others should go up to Jerusalem to the apostles and presbyters about this question... After much debate had taken place, Peter got up and said to them..." This is a description of the first Church council, held in

Jerusalem. Note that St. Paul did not attempt to settle the dispute by referring to "scripture alone." Instead, he defers to the authority of the Church. Also note that St. Peter settles the question after he has received—three times in fact—revelation in the form of a dream. (See Acts 11, where Peter explains the dream "step by step," just as popes today explain their teachings.) Clearly the Holy Spirit could not allow Peter to remain in error. When St. James speaks after Peter at the council, he is serving as moderator and summing up Peter's statement, since James is bishop of the city where the council is being held. Ever since, the bishops of the cities where councils are held have a ceremonial authority over the councils.

Mt. 10:2-4 – St. Peter is specified as "first" among the apostles: "The names of the twelve apostles are these: first, Simon called Peter..." Indeed, in every listing of the apostles, Peter is named first, and Judas last. We know why Judas was listed last. Can anyone claim that Peter's position—first—is without significance?

Acts 12:5 – "...Prayer by the church was fervently being made..." for St. Peter when he was in prison. No other apostle was graced in this extraordinary way, with the entire Church in prayer—not even St. Paul.

Jn. 21:15-17 – Three times Jesus asks St. Peter: "Do you love me?..." and three times he commands Peter to "feed my lambs" and "tend my sheep." Note that Jesus makes no such request of any other apostle.

Mt. 17:24-27 – St. Peter is supplied with supernatural means to accomplish the task Jesus gives him: "...go to the sea, drop in a hook, and take the first fish that comes up. Open his mouth and you will find a coin worth twice the temple tax. Give that to them for me and for you." Peter, in paying the tax for Jesus, acts as the Lord's proxy in this earthly matter.

Mt. 14:28-33 – St. Peter is the one who walks on water, through faith; when he falters, Jesus reaches out to him and saves him. The history of the Church would suggest that this arrangement is ongoing.

Lk 5:1-3 – St. Peter is called by Jesus; the boat and the nets are Peter's. "Getting into one of the boats, the one belonging to Simon, he asked him to put out a short distance from the shore." This is the source of the Church's nickname, "the barque of St. Peter." *Barque* is an archaic word for a small boat. In St. Peter's boat, the Lord himself is riding.

Acts 1:15-26 – St. Peter initiates and then supervises the choice of Judas' successor. "During those days Peter stood up in the midst of the brothers..."

Acts 3:1-10 – St. Peter performs the first miracle we see in scripture after Jesus' Ascension: "Peter said, 'I have neither silver nor gold, but what I do have, I give to you: in the name of Jesus Christ the Nazorean, [rise and] walk.' Then Peter took him by the right hand and raised him up, and immediately his feet and ankles grew strong. He leaped up..."

Acts 4:8-12 – When St. Peter and St. John are arrested, Peter is inspired by the Holy Spirit and speaks for them. "Then Peter, filled with the Holy Spirit, answered them..."

Acts 5:3-11 – When St. Peter condemns Ananias for dishonesty, Ananias dies: "...Peter said, 'Ananias, why has Satan filled your heart so that you lied to the Holy Spirit...?' When Ananias heard these words, he fell down and breathed his last, and great fear came upon all who heard of it." We see very early God acting upon St. Peter's injunctions. His words have authority on earth and in heaven (see Mt. 16:15-19, the first passage discussed in this section).

Acts 5:15 – "Thus they even carried the sick out into the streets and laid them on cots and mats so that when Peter came by, at least his shadow might fall on one or another of them." This is a striking manifestation of the healing power of St. Peter's mere presence.

Acts 8:9-25 – St. Peter pronounces judgment on Simon the Magician: "But Peter said to him, 'May your money perish with you...'" Simon is thrown into great fear because of Peter's admonition and he repents. He knows the authority by which St. Peter is speaking.

Acts 9:36-43 – St. Peter restores Tabitha, who was dead, to life. "Peter sent them all out and knelt down and prayed. Then he turned to her body and said, 'Tabitha, rise up.' She opened her eyes, saw Peter, and sat up." Again, God's power upholds Peter's actions.

Acts 9:32-35 – St. Peter heals Aeneas: "Peter said to him, 'Aeneas, Jesus Christ heals you. Get up and make your bed.' He got up at once."

Acts 10:9-43 – St. Peter receives a vision of the Gentiles' acceptance into the Church—remitting the circumcision requirement—*three times* before he yields. The Holy Spirit simply will not let Peter remain in ignorance or error: "Then Peter proceeded to speak and said, 'In truth, I see that God shows no partiality. Rather, in every nation whoever fears him and acts uprightly is acceptable to him.'" This is a vivid and immediate illustration of infallibility. Note that it was St. Peter who was the object of this supernatural intervention—not St. Paul, who was at the heart of the controversy, nor St. James, who was Bishop of Jerusalem where the First Council was to be held. Peter needed to give his assent before the Church could promulgate the teaching.

Mt. 23:1-3 – Jesus acknowledges the authority of even the Pharisees when they speak from the Chair of Moses: "...Jesus spoke to the crowds and to his disciples, saying, 'The scribes and the Pharisees have taken their seat on the chair of Moses. Therefore, do and observe all things whatsoever they tell you, but do not follow their example.'" Incidentally, the phrase, "the chair of Moses," is not found anywhere in the Old Testament. The fact that the Lord refers to it here confirms the fact that Jesus acknowledged the authority of tradition.

Out of 265 Popes, 79 were saints, only 10 were immoral or corrupt, and not one ever taught error in areas of faith or morals. That's a failure rate of less than 4 percent. By way of comparison, of the apostles picked by Jesus, one out of the original twelve was evil—representing a failure rate of 8 percent. So the supposed evil and corruption of the popes of history is hardly a reason to despair of the institution of the papacy. Indeed, we would suggest that the extremely low number of evil popes suggest Holy Spirit is guiding their selection and providing them support. Also, please note that the interpretations of the verses presented above are hardly novel. Witness this passage from Tertullian, written ca. 200 A.D.: "Was anything withheld from the knowledge of Peter, who is called, 'the rock on which the church should be built,' who also obtained 'the keys of the kingdom of heaven,' with the power of 'loosing and binding in heaven and on earth'?"(On Prescription against Heretics ANF 3:253). And from Origen, just two or three decades later, we find, "Look at that great foundation of the Church, that most solid of rocks upon whom Christ built the Church! And what does the Lord say to him? 'O you of little faith...'" (The Faith of the Early Fathers, Vol. 1, Willilam A. Jurgens, [Collegeville, Minnesota: Liturgical Press, 1970] p. 205).

APOSTOLIC SUCCESSION

The bishops of the Catholic Church can trace their ordinations back to the apostles themselves. This laying on of hands in the sacrament of Holy Orders takes place as part of an uninterrupted chain connecting us to Christ himself two thousand years ago. In every sense, today's bishops are the successors of Peter, Andrew, James, John, Philip, Bartholomew, Thomas, Matthew, James, Thaddaeus, Simon the Zealot and even—in very rare and unfortunate instances—to Judas Iscariot.

Acts 6:6 – "They presented these men to the apostles who prayed and laid hands on them." The Church's authority is thus passed from generation to generation.

Eph. 2:19-20 – "...household of God, built upon the foundation of the apostles and the prophets..." The Church's authority is not based on human wisdom or insight, or even on the Bible, but on the authority of God passed to and through the apostles.

1 Tim. 3:1 – "This saying is trustworthy: whoever aspires to the office of bishop desires a noble task." Note the reference to the episcopate as an "office." That clearly denotes an ongoing institution that is renewed from one generation to the next.

Acts 1:20-26 – "May another take his office." Peter supervises the choice of Judas' successor; Judas' spot did not die with him, it had to be filled. Therefore, Jesus wasn't just calling men to follow him when he appointed the apostles; he was establishing an ongoing "office" which was to be occupied from one generation to the next.

Acts 14:23 – St. Paul and St. Barnabas ordain others. No one ordains himself, nor does anyone presume to act as presbyter without first being ordained: "They appointed presbyters for them in each church..."

2 Tim. 1:6 – "I remind you to stir into flame the gift of God that you have through the imposition of my hands." The laying on of hands is the vehicle whereupon the Holy Spirit—the "flame"—is imparted. This is an utterly sacramental view of the infusion of the life of the Holy Spirit, and of the passing on of apostolic authority.

2 Tim. 2:1-2 – St. Paul commissions Timothy to carry on the work of the apostles: "So you, my child, be strong in the grace that is in Christ Jesus. And what you have heard from me through many witnesses entrust to faithful people who will have the ability to teach others as well." Paul here gives us an excellent insight into the workings of Sacred Tradition—the teachings of the apostles that are passed along, through the authority of the Church—from one generation to the next.

2 Tim. 3:14 – "...Remain faithful to what you have learned and believed, because you know from whom you learned it..." Authority is derived from apostolic succession—not from an appeal to "scripture alone." The Bible is quite clear on this.

Is. 22:15-25 – Eliakim is given the keys of the kingdom. Thus, he becomes "master of the palace," the second most powerful man in the realm, behind only the king himself, for he wields the authority of the king. Likewise, in Mt. 16:19, Jesus gives St. Peter the keys to the kingdom of heaven. It is in this authority that Peter's power to bind and to loose—in heaven as well as on earth—is founded.

Heb. 13:7 – "Remember your leaders who spoke the word of God to you. Consider the outcome of their way of life and imitate their faith." Again, the hierarchy is upheld.

Gal. 1:8 – "But even if we or an angel from heaven should preach to you a gospel other than the one that we preached to you, let that one be accursed! As we have said before, and now I say again, if anyone preaches to you a gospel other than the one that you received, let that one be accursed!" The truth of scriptural interpretation does not come from men, but from the Holy Spirit, through the apostles and their successors. We are not free to arrive at our own interpretations of the scriptures, apart from the apostles and the Church Jesus founded upon them. Indeed, the authority of the scriptures is derived from the apostles—which is to say, the Church—and not vice versa.

As any good dictionary will attest, the word, "priest," is derived from the word we find in scripture, "presbyter." In basic terms, the Catholic Church is still structured the way it was in apostolic times, as noted in the New Testament, with bishops, priests and deacons making up the ranks of the hierarchy.

ORDINATION AND PRIESTHOOD

Priests do not come between Jesus and us. They are in Jesus, and of Jesus, and with Jesus. The priestly function actually dates back through the New Testament, to the earliest Old Testament times, with Melchizedek who offered sacrifice on behalf of Abraham. As St. Cyprian of Carthage wrote around the year 250 A.D.: "If Christ Jesus, our Lord and God, is Himself the High Priest of God the Father; and if He offered Himself as a sacrifice to the Father; and if He commanded that this be done in commemoration of Himself—then certainly the priest, who imitates that which Christ did, truly functions in place of Christ." (The Faith of The Early Fathers, Vol. 1, William A. Jurgens, [Collegeville, Minnesota: Liturgical Press, 1970] pp. 232-33.)

Deut. 34:9 – "Now Joshua, son of Nun, was filled with the spirit of wisdom, since Moses had laid his hands upon him; and so the Israelites gave him their obedience, thus carrying out the Lord's command to Moses." The wisdom and the authority of the Holy Spirit are imparted through the laying on of hands by those already in authority. This is still the case today, as we see in the Sacrament of Holy Orders, which is conducted by a bishop, acting under the authority given to the apostles by Jesus himself.

Gen. 14:18 – "Melchizedek, king of Salem, brought out bread and wine, and being a priest of God Most High, he blessed Abram..." Why did Abraham need to be blessed by a man, when he was chosen by God to be the father of nations? In scripture, no one takes the mantle of spiritual authority upon himself. Even Moses, after being chosen by God, reports to "all the elders of the Israelites" to convince them of his call (Ex. 4:29-31). Likewise, Jesus himself is dedicated in the temple and baptized in the Jordan. In submitting to such sacramental rituals himself, Jesus is showing us that no one is outside of the divinely ordained spiritual authority of the Church.

Heb. 7:1-28 – "You are a priest forever according the order of Melchizedek... Jesus has become the guarantee of an [even] better covenant... he, because he remains forever, has a priesthood that does not pass away." Refers to:

Ps. 110:4 – "Like Melchizedek you are a priest forever..." The priesthood of the Lord is ongoing and eternal. And since the priesthood of individual men is based on the priesthood of Jesus, we know it is ongoing and eternal also.

Heb. 5:1-4 – The role of the priest is clear in scripture: "Every high priest is taken from among men and made their representative before God, to offer gifts and sacrifices for sins... No one takes this honor upon himself but only when called by God, just as Aaron was." Since the time of the mysterious and ancient Melchizedek, the faithful have relied on priests to represent the community before the altar of the Lord. As for those who claim an extraordinary call by God apart from the Church, don't believe them unless they can manifest supernatural works to support their assertion. For, while some in the Bible are called in an extraordinary manner, apart from the spiritual authority of the community—Moses and St. Paul, for example—God always validates their calling in one of two ways. First, he will give his anointed one supernatural power, as in the case of Moses. Or else he will inspire those in spiritual authority— i.e., the Church—to recognize the call as genuine and validate it, as in the case of St. Paul (Acts 13:1-3). So we must demand that those claiming spiritual authority based on a special call of God produce clearly supernatural manifestations—miracles—as evidence of their authority, or that their calling be affirmed and supported by the Church. Not even Jesus was exempt from this requirement (see the following passage).

Jn. 14:10-11 – "The words that I speak to you I do not speak on my own. The Father who dwells in me is doing his works. Believe me that I am in the Father and the Father is in me, or else believe because of the works themselves." Not even Jesus expects us to believe—on his word alone—his claim to have been anointed by God outside the hierarchy of the Levitical priesthood and the temple. Jesus himself provided astonishing, virtually continuous supernatural evidence of his status as Messiah, evidence that established beyond dispute the authority of his teaching. So why would we believe others—far less worthy individuals than Jesus—who also claim extraordinary calls but do not provide the clear and compelling evidence of miracles to affirm the heavenly origin of their mission?

Jn. 20:19-23 – At Pentecost, Jesus ordained the apostles and commissioned them to go out and minister to the world: "'As the Father has sent me, so I send you.' And when he had said this, he breathed on them and said to them, 'Receive the Holy Spirit. Whose sins you forgive are forgiven them, and whose sins you retain are retained.'" The fact that he sent them as the Father had sent him shows that he intends them to function as he did—as priests. It is no coincidence that it is here he also gives them the priestly power to forgive sins.

Acts 13:1-3 – Even the great St. Paul could not declare himself a minister of God—not even after the Lord had called him by name. He had to submit to the authority of the Church; he needed to be ordained: "Now there were in the church at Antioch prophets and teachers: Barnabas, Symeon who was called Niger, Lucius of Cyrene, Manaen who was a close friend of Herod the tetrarch, and Saul. While they were worshiping the Lord and fasting, the Holy Spirit said, 'Set apart for me Barnabas and Saul for the work to which I have called them.' Then, completing their fasting and prayer, they laid hands on them and sent them off."

Rom. 10:15 – "…How can people preach unless they are sent?" Even St. Paul needed to be "sent" by the Church (see the passage above). That's what ordination is—a "sending" through the imparting of the Holy Spirit through the laying on of hands. St. Paul is telling us here that no one can rightfully preach without submitting to and receiving the authority of the Church.

2 Tim. 1:6 – "I remind you to stir into flame the gift of God that you have through the imposition of my hands." St. Paul is clearly referring to a sacramental moment, when the Holy Spirit is imparted through the laying on of hands. This describes how priests are ordained even today.

Acts 6:6-7 – "They presented these men to the apostles who prayed and laid hands on them." Everywhere they went, the apostles ordained leaders for the community, imparting the Holy Spirit and the authority to carry on the work of the Church.

Acts 14:23 – St. Paul and St. Barnabas ordain others; no one ordains himself, nor does the community have the power to ordain: "They appointed presbyters for them in each church…"

Acts 8:9-25 – When Simon the Magician wished to receive the power of the Holy Spirit, he did not simply declare himself a minister and begin to preach. Instead, he approached St. Peter with his proposition. Even this sinner knew that he could not ordain or anoint himself.

1 Tim. 5:17 – "Presbyters who preside well deserve double honor, especially those who toil in preaching and teaching... Do not lay hands too readily on anyone..."

Heb. 6:2 – "...laying on of hands..."

Mal. 2:7 – "...The lips of the priest are to keep knowledge, and instruction is to be sought from his mouth, because he is the messenger of the Lord of hosts."

Phil. 1:1 – "...To all the holy ones in Christ Jesus, who are in Philippi, with the overseers and ministers." The Church hierarchy existed from the first Christian generation.

All of the faithful are "a royal priesthood, a holy nation" (1 Pet. 2:9), because we offer all we have and all we do to the service of the Lord. And we pray that our personal sacrifice is acceptable to him. But that does not mean we are authorized as individuals to offer Mass on behalf of the community. That privilege is set-aside for the men to whom the Holy Spirit has been imparted through the laying on of hands. It is no accident that we see no one in the early Church taking such authority upon themselves. In apostolic times, the authority to teach and preach was always imparted through the laying on of hands by the apostles.

SALVATION NOT BY FAITH ALONE/NOT ASSURED

Salvation is a gift from God made possible by the sacrifice of Christ Jesus. It is not won by our own actions or merits. To deny this truth is not Catholicism at all, but the ancient heresy of Pelagianism. Still, it does not follow from this that we will escape responsibility for the way we live out our commitment to faith, as the Protestant tradition claims. Each of us must decide whether to accept or reject the salvation which Jesus gained on our behalf—i.e., whether we will participate in God's plan for creation, or obstinately insist upon our own. We must say yes to God's call—actively and decisively—before we can enter into his eternal life. By contrast, Martin Luther taught that we are saved by "faith alone" and that no evil act we can ever commit will jeopardize our salvation. The Bible contradicts his position. St. Paul tells us in Rom. 6:23 that "the wages of sin is death." Below, you will find dozens more passages that refute Luther's false teaching. For the Bible states that while we are indeed saved by faith, it is not by "faith alone." We must live out our faith, through obedience, through perseverance, and through love. Where the Reformers erroneously drove a wedge between faith and good works, the Bible tells us they are inseparable.

James 1:22-25 – "Be doers of the word and not hearers only, deluding yourselves." James is clear: Our active participation in God's plan— our positive response to God's call to live out our faith—is required.

James 2:14-26 – "You believe that God is one. You do well. Even the demons believe that and tremble. Do you want proof, you ignoramus, that faith without works is useless?" James seems pretty definite that "faith alone" is not sufficient for salvation, for even the evil one and his minions have "faith alone." This passage stands as a ringing—and divinely inspired—refutation of Luther's erroneous doctrine. It is little wonder that Luther disputed the Epistle of James' place in the canon of the New Testament, referring to it as "an epistle of straw."

Mt. 25:31-46 – "...I was hungry and you gave me food, I was thirsty and you gave me drink, a stranger and you welcomed me, naked and you clothed me, ill and you cared for me, in prison and you visited me." At judgment, Jesus will acknowledge those who *live out* their faith by loving one another.

Mt. 7:21-23 – "Not everyone who says to me, 'Lord, Lord,' will enter the kingdom of heaven, but only the one who does the will of my Father in heaven. Many will say to me on that day, 'Lord, Lord, did we not prophesy in your name? Did we not drive out demons in your name? Did we not do mighty deeds in your name?' Then I will declare to them solemnly, 'I never knew you. Depart from me, you evildoers.'" Jesus is definite: Judgment will be based on how we live out our faith, not on "faith alone." For Jesus tells us those who *do* the Father's will are saved, and he condemns "evil*doers*," not "un*believe*rs." Precisely the same point is made in Luke 13:25-28.

Jn. 5:29 – "...All who are in the tombs will hear his voice and will come out, those who have done good deeds to the resurrection of life, but those who have done wicked deeds to the resurrection of condemnation." Judgment will depend on how we live out our faith. How could this simple fact be clearer in scripture?

Sir. 16:12-14 – "Great as his mercy is his punishment; he judges men, each according to his deeds... Whoever does good has his reward, which each receives according to his deeds." Again, what could be clearer?

Luke 10:25-28 – Here Jesus answers the question of salvation directly. A scholar asks, "'Teacher, what must I do to inherit eternal life?' Jesus said to him, 'What is written in the law? How do you read it?' He said in reply, 'You shall love the Lord, your God, with all your heart with all your being, with all your strength, and with all your mind, and your neighbor as yourself.' He replied to him, 'You have answered correctly; do this and you will live.'" This passage is definitive. Look at the question first. It reads: "What must I *do?*" Not "What must I *believe?*" And then examine Jesus' reply. He does not affirm Luther's principle—which states we are saved by "faith alone." He says we must *love*—which is itself an act; indeed, it is an act that presupposes a multitude of subsequent acts—or we will not be saved. Finally, don't miss the word "inherit." An inheritance is a gift that is given, not a wage that is earned. Our loving acts amount to our acceptance of our inheritance, which was gained for us by the sacrifice of Jesus, the lamb.

Rom. 2:13 – "For it is not those who hear the law who are just in the sight of God; rather, those who observe the law will be justified." "Faith alone"—simply hearing the law—is not enough to save us. Instead, we must commit ourselves to *observing* the law. Our actions are required— our positive response to God's call.

Rom. 2:5-11 – "...The just judgment of God, who will repay everyone according to his works." Paul is clear on this. We will be judged by our commitment to our faith. Which is not the same thing as saying that our salvation comes through our own deeds or merits, for—as the Church has always taught—without Jesus there would be no possibility of redemption.

Ezek. 33:13-14 – "Though I say to the virtuous man that he shall surely live, if he then presumes on his virtue and does wrong, none of his virtuous deeds shall be remembered; because of the wrong he has done, he shall die. And though I say to the wicked man that he shall surely die, if he turns away from his sin and does what is right and just, giving back pledges, restoring stolen goods, living by the statutes that bring life, and doing no wrong, he shall surely live, he shall not die." This verse states quite explicitly that we are judged on our actions, and nowhere does it mention "faith alone" being sufficient for salvation. Indeed, it does not mention faith at all. It also clearly rules out the Protestant doctrine of "eternal security," in which a one-time pronouncement of faith assures us of salvation, regardless of our subsequent actions. Again, this passage is not saying we "earn" our admission to eternal life apart from the sacrifice of Jesus. It is saying we are required to respond to God's call with our "obedience of faith," as St. Paul puts it. Failing that, we will not be saved. (See also the following three verses.)

Rom. 1:4-6 – Faith requires of us a response, an act of "obedience," as we see in this passage: "Through him [Jesus], we have received the grace of apostleship, to bring about the obedience of faith, for the sake of his name..." Faith results in a concrete change of life. We must obey our "faith" and submit our wills to God's. Through this phrase, "the obedience of faith," St. Paul inextricably links faith to good works.

Rom. 6:16 – Again, St. Paul refers to "obedience of faith." Note that St. Paul nowhere refers to "faith alone." Faith cannot exist in a vacuum. The truth is, there is no such thing as "faith alone," apart from obedience, apart from good works, apart from love. Faith implies—requires—all these things. "Faith alone" is not faith at all.

Rom. 16:26 – St. Paul's "obedience of faith" refers to a faith response—a life-changing commitment we make to the God who has saved us: "...the commandment of the eternal God...has been made known to all the nations, leading to obedience of faith..."

Ezek. 18:26-30 – "When a virtuous man turns away from virtue to commit iniquity, and dies, it is because of the iniquity he committed that he must die. But if a wicked man, turning from the wickedness he has committed, does what is right and just, he shall preserve his life; since he has turned away from all the sins that he committed, he shall surely live, he shall not die... Turn and be converted from all your crimes, that they may be no cause of guilt for you." Again, judgment is based on our actions as well as our faith, not on our "faith alone."

1 Cor. 13:2-3 – "...If I have all faith so as to move mountains but do not have love, I am nothing." Faith alone? Hmm. What about "love alone"?

Eph. 5:4-7 – "Be sure of this, that no immoral or impure or greedy person... has any inheritance in the kingdom..." Judgment will be based on more than just whether we believe, but on how we live out our beliefs. There are at least four other times in his letters that St. Paul condemns wrongdoers, saying that those who do such things "are deserving of death," that they will be subject to "the wrath of God" and that they will not "inherit the kingdom of God" (Rom 1:18-32; 1 Cor. 6:9-10; Gal. 5:19-21, and Col. 3:5-6). Note that Paul says nothing about the evildoers' faith; he refers only to their actions.

Rom. 3:28 – "For we maintain that a man is justified by faith apart from works of the law." Luther admitted adding "alone" to this verse in his Bible, rendering it, "...man is justified by faith *alone* apart from works of the law." But that is Luther's teaching, not God's. Indeed, we know that Rev. 22:18-19 condemns anyone who changes even one word of scripture. Also, examining the verse in context makes it clear that St. Paul is talking here about the Mosaic Law and the belief of many Jews that when they kept the external precepts of the law, God would be compelled to save them, regardless of their arrogance and hardness of heart. Paul is pointing out their error. No act is good if it is not accompanied by—and motivated by—love. St. John puts it like this:

1 Jn. 3:21-24 – "Beloved, if [our] hearts do not condemn us, we have confidence in God and receive from him whatever we ask, because we keep his commandments and do what pleases him." Faith, love and good actions are inseparable.

Rom. 6:23 – "...The wages of sin is death..." In Luther's theology, no actions—neither sin nor good works—can in any way affect our salvation. This stems from his flawed interpretation of Rom. 3:28 (see above). But his theology contradicts this verse, also from Romans. Thus, we have clear evidence of Luther's error, since we know the Bible cannot contradict itself.

2 Cor. 5:10 – "For we must all appear before the judgment seat...so that each one may receive recompense, according to what he did in the body, whether good or evil." "Faith alone" isn't enough; we must live out our faith.

Lk. 8:13 – "...They believe only for a time and fall away..." One of the main points of the parable of the sower and the seed is that salvation is *not* assured. When we opt for evil—placing our will above God's—we forfeit the salvation Jesus gained for us.

Phil. 2:12 – "...Work out your salvation in fear and trembling..." St. Paul is again clear: Salvation is not assured. For we may at any time succumb to temptation and reject God and his plan for our life.

1 Jn. 3:7 – "Children, let no one deceive you. The person who acts in righteousness is righteous..." The person who *acts*, not the person who simply believes. Our active participation in—and commitment to—our faith is absolutely necessary.

Acts 10:34-35 – "In truth, I see that God shows no partiality. Rather, in every nation whoever fears him and acts uprightly is acceptable to him." It seems that more than our faith is assessed by God in determining who is righteous.

James 1:4 – "And let perseverance be perfect, so that you may be perfect and complete, lacking in nothing." We must persevere in the struggle for salvation while we are on earth. If we were totally assured of salvation in this life, this verse about "perseverance" would be meaningless.

Mt. 19:16-21 – "Go and sell your possessions..." The rich young man did not fail the test because of a lack of faith, but rather because he did not *act* on his faith. His faith was not lacking, his works were.

Mt. 5:19-20 – "Therefore, whoever breaks one of the least of these commandments and teaches others to do so will be called the least in the kingdom of heaven. But whoever obeys and teaches those commandments will be called greatest in the kingdom of heaven. I tell you, unless your righteousness surpasses that of the scribes and Pharisees, you will not enter into the kingdom of heaven." Actions seem to be important to Jesus. He expects us to keep the commandments, even though he also knows his death will atone for all sins.

Mt. 6:1-4 – "...Take care not to perform righteous deeds in order that people may see them; otherwise you will have no recompense from your heavenly Father. When you give alms, do not blow a trumpet before you, as the hypocrites do in the synagogues and in the streets to win the praise of others. Amen, I say to you, they have received their reward. But when you give alms, do not let your left hand know what your right is doing, so that your almsgiving may be secret. And your Father who sees in secret will repay you." If doing good works is of no consequence, then why does Jesus tell us that the Father will repay us when we do them?

Heb. 10:26-29 – "If we sin deliberately after receiving knowledge of the truth, there no longer remains sacrifice for sins but a fearful prospect of judgment and a flaming fire that is going to consume the adversaries. Anyone who rejects the Law of Moses is put to death without pity on the testimony of two or three witnesses. Do you not think that a much worse punishment is due the one who has contempt for the Son of God...?" We will be punished for our sins more severely than those who sinned before Jesus' coming.

2 Pet. 1:5-11 – "Therefore, brothers, be all the more eager to make your call and election firm." Salvation is not guaranteed; we must do our best to preserve it. Also, St. Peter is indicating that the firmness of our election depends on us—and our response to the call of God—and not on the Lord's sacrifice alone. Thus we see that faith is itself, in the way most Protestants use the term, a "work."

1 Cor. 4:4-5 – "...I do not thereby stand acquitted; the one who judges me is the Lord. Therefore, do not make any judgment before the appointed time..." Salvation is not assured, even for St. Paul.

1 Cor. 9:27 – "...For fear that, after having preached to others, I myself should be disqualified." St. Paul is not absolutely assured of his own salvation. How could we possibly presume to be assured of ours?

1 Cor. 10:12 – "...Whoever thinks he is standing secure should take care not to fall." St. Paul is clear: Our salvation is not assured. It hangs in the balance, and how we conduct our lives—the commitment we make to our faith, which we have received through the grace of God—will determine our ultimate disposition.

Gal. 5:6 – St. Paul makes it clear that what counts is "...faith working through love." Hardly "faith alone."

2 Tim. 2:11-12 – "If we have died with him we shall also live with him; if we persevere we shall also reign with him." Salvation is not based on "faith alone." Free gift that it is, faith must nonetheless lead to a life-changing commitment, which requires perseverance, as St. Paul observes. The conditional "if" ought not be ignored here.

Rom. 3:25 – Scripture gives us no indication that our sins are forgiven prior to our committing them: "...because of the forgiveness of sins previously committed..." "Previously committed" not "committed in the future" or "committed for all time."

1 Jn. 3:10 – "In this way, the children of God and the children of the devil are made plain; no one who fails to act in righteousness belongs to God, nor anyone who does not love his brother." Again it would seem that "love alone" is a more apt description of what is required for salvation than "faith alone." We are revealed as "children of the devil" not by a lack of faith, but by a lack of righteous and loving actions.

1 Jn. 5:2-4 – "For the love of God is this, that we keep his commandments." Not that we have "faith alone."

2 Pet. 2:20-21 – "For if they, having escaped the defilements of the world... again become entangled and overcome by them, their last condition is worse than their first." So we see that those who were "once saved" are not in fact "always saved."

Jn. 3:5 – "...No one can enter the kingdom...without being born of water and the Spirit..." Baptism is required for salvation, not simply "faith alone." And in truth, drawing a distinction between Baptism and faith would have not made sense to the early Christians. They saw them as inextricably related—neither was complete without the other.

Lk. 18:9-14 – The parable of the prayers of the Pharisee and the tax collector; Christ tells us that "faith alone" is not sufficient for salvation. The Pharisee had much faith, but he committed the sin of pride and offended God. His "faith alone" was not enough to save him.

Mt. 18:32-35 – "Then in anger his master handed him over to the torturers until he should pay back the whole debt. So will my heavenly Father do to you, unless each of you forgives his brother from his heart." Jesus is telling us that the "work" of forgiving one another is required for salvation.

1 Cor. 4:4-5 – "...Do not make any judgment before the appointed time..." St. Paul is telling us clearly that salvation is not eternally assured.

Rom. 11:22 – "...Provided you remain in his kindness; otherwise you too will be cut off." Salvation is not assured until judgment. This is true even for those who are baptized, for the community St. Paul is writing to here is made up of believers.

Rom. 5:2 – "...We boast in hope of the glory of God." If salvation were assured, we would have more than just "hope." We would have certainty.

Rom. 8:24-25 – "...If we hope for what we do not see, we wait with endurance." Our salvation is *not* totally assured. We must endure.

Lk. 13:6-9 – "...It may bear fruit in the future. If not you can cut it down." We must bear fruit in this life—i.e., we must work to further God's plan—or we risk being cut down. What will insure that we bear fruit? Not "faith alone," but a life-changing commitment to our faith.

Heb. 6:4-8 – "For it is impossible in the case of those who have once been enlightened and tasted the heavenly gift and shared in the holy Spirit and tasted the good word of God and the powers of the age to come, and then have fallen away, to bring them to repentance again, since they are recrucifying the Son of God for themselves and holding him up to contempt." Salvation is not assured.

Gal. 6:6-10 – "...Let us not grow tired of doing good..." Our actions do matter, which is why St. Paul is constantly exhorting his followers to do good.

2 Cor. 9:6 – "Consider this: whoever sows sparingly will also reap sparingly, and whoever sows bountifully will also reap bountifully." St. Paul is calling us to give generously of ourselves and our possessions.

Rom. 7:6 – The Ten Commandments sum up the natural law—nothing more. Keeping the Ten Commandments—and the entirety of the Mosaic law—was never enough for salvation: "But now we are released from the law, dead to what held us captive, so that we may serve in the newness of the spirit..." We are called to do more than simply avoid evil. We must respond positively to Jesus' call to love God and one another.

Rom. 8:13 – "For if you live according to the flesh, you will die, but if by the spirit you put to death the deeds of the body, you will live." Once again St. Paul tells us that we will be judged by our actions.

Mk. 8:34 – "Whoever wishes to come after me must deny himself, take up his cross and follow me." Taking up one's cross involves much more than just faith. Faith is of course the basis, but strength, courage, perseverance, self-denial and love are also required.

Rev. 21:7-8 – "But as for cowards, the unfaithful, the depraved...their lot is in the burning pool of fire..." God judges our actions. Our faith *must* bear good fruit. It will, provided we cooperate with the graces offered us by God and unite our wills to his.

Mk. 14:38 – "Watch and pray that you not enter into temptation." Salvation is not assured until judgment, because at any time we may "enter into temptation" and fall into sin.

Mt. 10:22 – "...whoever endures to the end will be saved." Our salvation is not fully and totally assured. Our endurance—our perseverance—is required.

Rom. 6:16 – Justification is a process we continually anticipate: "...you are slaves of the one you obey, either of sin, which leads to death, or of obedience, which leads to righteousness." Justification is not something accomplished once, in the past. We see by the tense of the verb, "leads," that it is ongoing, continuing throughout our lives.

Mt. 12:36 – Not only our actions, but even our words will help determine our judgment: "I tell you, on the day of judgment, people will render an account for every careless word they speak. By your words you will be acquitted, and by your words you will be condemned."

Gal. 5:4-5 – Justification is a process we await: "...we await the hope of righteousness." Justification is not a once-for-all occurrence. It happened in the past. It is happening now. It will happen in the future—all provided we respond positively to the free gift of God's call.

Gal. 2:17 – Justification is not permanent, not assured: "But if, in seeking to be justified in Christ, we ourselves are found to be sinners, is Christ then a minister of sin? Of course not!" Some who may consider themselves to be "saved" will in fact be "found to be sinners."

Rom. 3:24 – St. Paul refers to justification in the present tense: "They are justified freely by his grace..." So justification is clearly an ongoing process that takes place in the past, present and future. It is not the "once-saved-always-saved" proposition that so many preach.

1 Cor. 1:18 – Again, justification is said to be ongoing; Paul refers to it in the present tense: "The message of the cross is foolishness to those who are perishing, but to us who are being saved it is the power of God."

Jn. 3:19-21 – "For everyone who does wicked things hates the light and does not come toward the light, so that his works might not be exposed." Evil actions separate us from the light.

Tob. 4:21 – "...Avoid all sin, and do what is right before the Lord your God." What we *do* matters, as well as what we believe. We are required to live out our faith by acting uprightly.

Mt. 9:20 – "A woman suffering hemorrhages for twelve years came up behind him and touched the tassel on his cloak. She said to herself, 'If only I can touch his cloak, I will be cured'..." "Faith alone" had not healed the suffering woman. She had to step forward in faith and *touch* the cloak. It was her faith in Jesus combined with her action, that yielded the cure.

Gal 5:5 – In his letters, many of St. Paul's references to "the law" pertain to the Jews' efforts to justify themselves through the practices of the old law, apart from the saving power of Jesus' sacrifice: "For in Christ Jesus, neither circumcision nor uncircumcision counts for anything, but only faith working through love." What Paul is *not* saying is that the faithful are absolved from the requirements of responding to God's call, or of following Jesus' law of love. He is simply pointing out that being born Jewish does not assure one of salvation. The rituals and practices of the old covenant—or what it means to "be a Jew"—have been superseded by Jesus' law of love, which is written on our hearts, not on stone tablets. (See below:)

2 Cor. 3:3 – "You are our letter, written on our hearts, known and read by all, shown to be a letter of Christ administered by us, written not in ink but by the Spirit of the living God, not on tablets of stone but on tablets that are hearts of flesh." This is a magnificent passage that indicates the immediacy of Christ's law of love in our lives. It must not remain an outside influence, but be incorporated into our very being. This passage does *not* mean that we believers can ignore the law and act as we please, injuring and abusing others without jeopardizing our salvation, which is the interpretation of Protestants who hold to the doctrine of "assured salvation."

2 Cor. 9:10 – "The one who supplies seed to the sower and bread for food will supply and multiply your seed and increase the harvest of your righteousness." Our good works are clearly not ours alone, but evidence of God working through us. To deny their significance is to render our lives meaningless and the lessons we learn superfluous.

Col. 1:24 – "Now I rejoice in my sufferings for your sake, and in my flesh I am filling up what is lacking in the afflictions of Christ..." What could Jesus' suffering have possibly lacked? One thing only: the free and positive response of the individual soul to the Holy Spirit's call. Jesus could not make a committed faith response for St. Paul—i.e., he could not save Paul against his will—and he doesn't respond for us either. This is why "faith alone" is not enough to save us, and it's why even Jesus' perfect sacrifice does not save every individual either. Jesus redeemed us, making us adopted sons of the Father and opening the doors of heaven to us. It is up to us to decide whether we will accept or refuse that redemption— whether we will walk through those wide-swinging doors and accept our inheritance.

*From its earliest days, the Church has taught that individuals, having been saved by Jesus' sacrifice, would be judged on their response to the call of faith in their lives. Around the year 200 A.D., St. Clement of Alexandria wrote: "When we hear, 'Your faith has saved you,' we do not understand the Lord to say simply that they will be saved who have believed in whatever manner, even if works have not followed" (*The Faith of the Early Fathers, *Vol. 1, William A. Jurgens [Collegeville, Minnesota: Liturgical Press, 1970] p. 184.) As is so often the case, the early community dispensed with a question that would later confuse and bedevil separated Christians for centuries. If we ignore the teachings of these early giants who lived under the very shadow of the apostles, we do so at our peril. Compare the passages above, in which we see the scriptures constantly urging the faithful to holiness and uprightness, to the following paragraph taken from a letter written by Martin Luther to his follower, Philip Melancthon, in which he states: "Be a sinner, and let your sins be strong, but let your trust in Christ be stronger, and rejoice in Christ who is the victor over sin, death, and the world. We will commit sins while we are here, for this life is not a place where justice resides... No sin can separate us from Him, even if we were to kill or commit adultery thousands of times each day." ("Let Your Sins Be Strong", from* The Wittenberg Project; The Wartburg Segment, *translated by Erika Flores, from Dr. Martin Luther's "Saemmtliche Schriften", Letter No. 99, 1 Aug. 1521.) Nowhere in this letter does Luther mention contrition or repentance, for repentance is itself a "work," and Luther's theology of salvation leaves no room for good works. Instead, here Luther is actually urging his followers to sin as a sign of their faith. The perversity of such a theology is stunning—one reason, perhaps, that unedited editions of Luther's writings are not widely available.*

DOCTRINES

The Church, from its earliest days in Jerusalem, has often found it necessary to define doctrines, either to clarify teachings or to settle disputes. Not one of these doctrines in any way contradicts scripture; they only verify it and clarify it, as was true in apostolic times.

Acts 15 – St. Paul and St. Barnabas take the Church's dogmas—as defined by the Council of Jerusalem—to Antioch. An interesting note here: They did not feel compelled to justify these dogmas by appealing to the scriptures. They clearly considered their apostolic authority to be sufficient.

Acts 16:4 – "As they traveled from city to city, they handed on to the people for observance the decisions reached by the apostles and presbyters in Jerusalem." St. Paul and St. Timothy take the dogmas of the early Church to the world. Apparently they did not feel that all Christians would spontaneously perceive the truth simply through a personal reading of the scriptures. They found it necessary to instruct the faithful concerning these truths, just as the Church does today.

Many people object to the idea of doctrines being defined by a spiritual authority, thinking that they intrude upon personal spirituality. These individuals yearn for simplicity of an idealized, streamlined Christianity, something along the lines of, "Jesus loves us, and he just wants us to love one another." But such a thing is of course impossible, since every truth of our faith opens up a world of questions. Such as, "Who is Jesus" and, "Why does he love us" and "What does it mean, really, to love another human being?" Jesus himself seems to acknowledge the quandary of not knowing what one believes as he addresses the Samaritan woman at the well. He tells her: "You worship what you do not know; we worship what we know, for salvation is from the Jews"(Jn. 4:22). It is better to worship what one knows.

FREE WILL

A fundamental difference between Catholic and Protestant theology is the belief in free will, which both Luther and Calvin deny. Because of the doctrine of "sola fide"—that faith alone is sufficient for salvation—the Reformers taught that the individual does not cooperate in his or her salvation in any way. According to them, every moral choice is predetermined. By contrast, Catholics believe that, because man was created in God's image, we are given the opportunity to accept or reject God's grace. Like the angels, we may choose either to follow God's will, or we may elect to turn to our own selfish inclinations—in other words, to sin. The choice is ours. And this is the great gift that sprang from Christ's redemptive sacrifice—to freely participate in the building of the kingdom. Without Jesus, we would have no chance to accept our place as God's children. Of course which path we choose is of the utmost importance to creation. For no one else can take our unique place in it or accomplish what is ours to accomplish.

Deut. 30:19-20 – "I have set before you life and death, the blessing and the curse. Choose life, then, that you and your descendants may live, by loving the Lord, your God, heeding his voice, and holding fast to him." Man is more than free to choose; he is obliged to choose.

Gen. 4:7 – God tells Cain he can defeat sin if he wills it: "Why are you so resentful and crestfallen? If you do well, you can hold up your head; but if not, sin is a demon lurking at the door: his urge is toward you, yet you can be his master."

Rom. 7:21 – "...When I want to do right, evil is at hand." St. Paul indicates the problem is with our wills, not our destinies.

Sir. 15:11-20 – "Say not: 'It was God's doing that I fell away;' for what he hates he does not do. Say not: 'It was he who set me astray;' for he has no need of wicked men... When God, in the beginning, created man, he made him subject to his own free choice. If you choose you can keep the commandments... There are set before you fire and water; to whichever you choose, stretch forth your hand." Here we see an explicit affirmation of the Church's teaching on free will.

1 Cor. 10:13 – "No trial has come to you but what is human. God is faithful and will not let you be tried beyond your strength; but with the trial he will also provide a way out, so that you may be able to bear it."

James 1:13-15 – "No one experiencing temptation should say, 'I am being tempted by God;' for God is not subject to temptation to evil, and he himself tempts no one. Rather, each person is tempted when he is lured and enticed by his own desire." With this passage, James seems to put the matter to rest.

Prov. 1:24 – "...I called and you refused, I extended my hand and no one took notice..." God invites us. He does not compel us.

2 Pet. 3:9 – "The Lord...is patient with you, not wishing that any should perish but that all should come to repentance." The fact that not all do come to repentance—despite God's wish that they would—proves conclusively that we are capable of deciding whether to accept or reject God's will, which of course is the essence of free will.

Jn. 6:37 – "...I will not reject anyone who comes to me." Jesus promises to accept those of us who accept him. He has made his overtures to every person ever created.

Ex. 8:15 – "Pharaoh remained obstinate... just as the Lord had foretold." God did not overwhelm Pharaoh's will and cause him to do evil. God simply knew Pharaoh's actions ahead of time.

Ezek. 18:23 – "Do I indeed derive any pleasure from the death of the wicked? says the Lord God. Do I not rather rejoice when he turns from his evil way that he may live?" The choice of good and evil is ours to make. God desires us to do good, but he does not compel us.

Gal. 2:17 – When we sin, it is our doing, not God's: "But if, in seeking to be justified in Christ, we ourselves are found to be sinners, is Christ then a minister of sin? Of course not!" Again we see St. Paul cutting to the chase here. We are the sinners, not Christ.

Ps. 5:5 – "You are not a god who delights in evil..." God cannot will evil. Yet the doctrine of predestination requires us to believe he does. Those who believe in it must view God as author of evil as well as good—an utterly monstrous theology.

2 Tim. 2:11-13 – "...If we persevere we shall also reign with him. But if we deny him he will deny us." St. Paul tells us our salvation depends on what path we decide to take—toward God or away from him.

Rom. 1:20-21 – "Ever since the creation of the world, his invisible attributes of eternal power and divinity have been able to be understood and perceived in what he has made. As a result, they have no excuse; for although they knew God they did not accord him glory as God or give him thanks." God's glory is evident to all, but not all choose to acknowledge it.

1 Sam. 23:9-13 – David, embroiled in a struggle with Saul, specifically asks God about events in the future. He asks if Saul is coming to Keilah to kill him, and God answers, "He will come down." Whereupon David asks whether the citizens of the city will hand him over to Saul to be killed, and God responds, "Yes." We know that God is all knowing and incapable of deceit. So God is telling David precisely what he foresees—David's death at the hands of Saul. This is not a simple prediction, but the description of a reality that will unquestionably occur, should conditions remain the same; it is a statement of the future that comes from the mind of God, who can see not just the future, as it will unfold, but also every possible future that *could* occur but will not. Yet God's prediction, which we know must have been true when he spoke it, does not in fact come to pass. Why? Because when David takes the information and decides to follow a different path himself—collecting his followers and leaving Keilah—the future changes. Saul does not come into Keilah after all, and David is not handed over to him. Thus, David, by exercising his will, actually changes the events of the future. God's foreknowledge does not impinge upon David's freedom. On the contrary, David's actions—formed and guided by his own free will—determine the events of the future. This is a measure of the great gift God has given us—namely, to take part in the shaping of creation. *The early Church fathers disposed of the error of predestination in short order. Eusebius Pamphillus wrote in about 315 A.D.:"...foreknowledge of events is not the cause of the occurrence of those events...not because it is known does it take place; but because it is about to take place, it is known." (*The Faith of the Early Fathers,*'Vol. 1, William A. Jurgens, [Collegeville, Minnesota: Liturgical Press, 1970] p. 296.) And St. Augustine, in his uniquely clear and cogent manner, adds this thought in about 390 A.D.: "Just as you do not, by your memory of them, compel past events to have happened, neither does God, by His foreknowledge, compel future events to take place." (*The Faith of the Early Church Fathers,*'Vol. 3, William A. Jurgens, [Collegeville, Minnesota: Liturgical Press, 1970] p. 39).*

ABORTION

The Catholic Church's stand against abortion—taken in the face of unrelenting pressures from many interest groups—is one of the signs of the ongoing guidance of the Holy Spirit. It is one of the real points of departure between the Catholic Church and nearly every strain of American Protestantism. This divergence is proof, among other things, that the Protestant communities do not balk at changing their teachings when they deem it necessary. Remember that, until well into the twentieth century, not a single Christian tradition taught that abortion was permissible. And today, any faith community that has yielded on this issue has a major problem calling itself a scripture-based church. For there are many statements in the scriptures that indicate that the pre-natal individual is to be regarded as a human being:

Ps. 139:13 – "You formed my inmost being; you knit me in my mother's womb. I praise you, so wonderfully you made me... My very self you knew; my bones were not hidden from you, when I was being made in secret, fashioned as in the depths of the earth. Your eyes foresaw my actions; in your book all are written down; my days were shaped, before one came to be." Clearly, we are known to God as individuals even before we draw our first breath. Abortion wrenches the living individual out of earthly existence, and out of the vision of the future that exists in the mind of God.

Jer. 1:5 – "Before I formed you in the womb I knew you. Before you were born I dedicated you..." This is a powerful statement. God claims us as his own and sets our lives in motion from the very first moment of conception.

Eccles. 11:5 – "Just as you know not how the breath of life fashions the human frame in the mother's womb, so you know not the work of God which he is accomplishing in the universe."

Job 31:15 – "Did not he who made me in the womb make him? Did not the same One fashion us before our birth?" Note that Job says God fashions *us* in the womb, not indistinct, unspecialized fetal tissue that will later *become* us at birth.

Gen. 9:5 – "...From man in regard to his fellow man I will demand an accounting for human life." Life belongs to God. When we take it, we are not only robbing the individual whose life we take, but God as well.

Is. 49:1 – "The Lord called me from birth, from my mother's womb he gave me my name." We are individuals, known, loved and "named" by God, even from conception. Recall the importance of naming to the Hebrews. They believed that, in a very real sense, our essences — our beings—were reflected by our names. Hence the great significance when holy men like Abram, Jacob and Simon were given new names. And don't forget the power that the very name of God possessed. This verse, then, shows that an individual was regarded as whole and complete, even from conception.

Ps. 51:7 – "...I was born guilty, a sinner, even as my mother conceived me." We see that conception is in some sense a birth to our spiritual existence. This passage is also an affirmation of the doctrine of original sin.

Lk. 1:15 – "He will be filled with the Holy Spirit even from his mother's womb..." St. John the Baptist was filled with the Spirit long before he was born. By definition, he was a fully vested human person, with a body and a soul.

Lk. 1:41 – "When Elizabeth heard Mary's greeting, the infant leaped in her womb..." Even from the womb, St. John was able to respond to the promptings of the Holy Spirit. Note that Elizabeth's womb is said to be inhabited by an "infant" rather than a "fetus."

Lev. 20:10-12 – "If a man disgraces his father by lying with his father's wife, both the man and his stepmother shall be put to death; they have forfeited their lives. If a man lies with his daughter-in-law, both of them shall be put to death; since they have committed an abhorrent deed, they have forfeited their lives." Penalties for adultery and incest are death for the perpetrators, but not for the children that might be conceived through such acts. The children are innocent.

Lev. 18:21 – "You shall not offer any of your offspring to be immolated to Molech, thus profaning the name of your God." Abortion sacrifices children to the idols of money, convenience, and career.

1 Cor. 6:19 – A woman's right to control her body is superseded by God's claim on her being, both body and soul: "Do you not know that your body is a temple of the Holy Spirit within you, whom you have from God, and that you are not your own?"

Ps. 127:3 – "Children too are a gift from the Lord, the fruit of the womb, a reward." Any couple that has encountered difficulty conceiving knows firsthand what a gift it is to bring new life into existence.

*Abortion doesn't just kill the individual. It also destroys every thought the person would have ever had, every action the person would have ever undertaken, every contribution to the kingdom the person would have ever made. In short, abortion tears a piece out of the fabric of creation by destroying God's plan for a person's life, and the lives of the person's descendents. The earliest community of faith explicitly forbade abortion. In one of the most ancient non-scriptural documents of the Church, the Didache, we find this absolute and unequivocal admonition: "You shall not procure abortion, nor destroy a new-born child." (*The Faith of the Early Fathers, *Vol. 1, William A. Jurgens, [Collegeville, Minnesota: Liturgical Press, 1970] p. 2.)*

CONTRACEPTION

Rom. 1:26 – "Their females exchanged natural relations for unnatural... " The Bible makes it clear: There are in fact unnatural sexual relations possible between human beings. This is a point disputed by our culture, where the doctrine of "consenting adults" prevails. The "consenting adults" doctrine states that, to be permissible, any behavior needs only to be desired. So the simple fact of wanting to engage in a behavior automatically justifies it. Thus, in the eyes of our world, lust has supplanted children as the overarching value of sexual relations.

Ps. 127:3-5 – "Children too are a gift from the Lord..."

Gen. 30:22 – God remembers Rachel and gives her the gift of a son.

Gen. 9:7 – "'Be fertile, then, and multiply...'"

When sexuality is separated from procreation, it becomes self-directed and exploitative. All of the abuses against women and against life that Pope Paul VI predicted would result from contraception have come to pass in our culture—with a vengeance. (In his prophetic 1968 papal encyclical "Humanae Vitae" we find these words: "It is...to be feared that the man, growing used to the employment of anticontraceptive practices, may finally lose respect for the woman and, no longer caring for her physical and psychological equilibrium, may come to the point of considering her as a mere instrument of selfish enjoyment, and no longer as his respected and beloved companion." [Pauline

Books & Media, p.8].) Who can deny that our culture has gone down that precise path?

HOMOSEXUALITY

Rom. 1:27 – Every time homosexuality is referred to in the Bible, it is unequivocally condemned: "Males did shameful things with males..."

1 Cor. 6:9 – "Do you not know that the unjust will not inherit the kingdom of God? Do not be deceived; neither fornicators nor idolaters nor adulterers nor boy prostitutes nor sodomites nor thieves nor the greedy nor drunkards nor slanderers nor robbers will inherit the kingdom of God." Homosexual relations are said by St. Paul to be a deadly sin.

1 Tim. 1:8-11 – "We know that the law is good, provided that one uses it as law, with the understanding that law is meant not for a righteous person but for the lawless and unruly, the godless and sinful, the unholy and profane, those who kill their fathers or mothers, murderers, the unchaste, sodomites, kidnapers, liars, perjurers, and whatever else is opposed to sound teaching..." Homosexual acts are listed with the most serious of offenses.

Lev. 20:13 – "If a man lies with a male as with a woman, both of them shall be put to death for their abominable deed; they have forfeited their lives." The teaching here could not be clearer. Homosexual acts are a deadly sin.

The early Church likewise forbade homosexual acts. In the Didache, one of the earliest examples of non-scriptural Christian writings, we find these unequivocal proscriptions: "You shall not murder. You shall not commit adultery. You shall not seduce boys..." ('The Faith of the Early Fathers,' *Vol. 1, William A. Jurgens [Collegeville, Minnesota: Liturgical Press, 1970] p. 2.) Of course the fact that homosexuality is sinful does not mean those who suffer that particular temptation are any less children of God than those who are tempted in other directions. It is the act that is sinful, not the temptation or the "orientation." There is not a person who has ever lived who has not been tempted to sin. Judging others is no less sinful than homosexual acts.*

DIVORCE

The moral laxity that so many Protestant congregations have fallen into— permitting at-will divorce, contraception, homosexuality, abortion—is a terrible tragedy, and we Catholics ought to pray diligently for our brethren in faith. Since this laxity flies in the face of so many clear Bible teachings—many coming from the lips of Jesus himself—it is a further sign that the fullness of truth is not found in the Protestant tradition.

1 Cor. 7:10-11 – "To the married, however, I give this instruction (not I, but the Lord): a wife should not separate from her husband—and if she does separate she must either remain single or become reconciled to her husband—and a husband should not divorce his wife." St. Paul is resolute on the topic. Remarriage following the separation of a married couple—in other words, divorce—is not to be permitted.

Mt. 19:3-9 – "…They are no longer two, but one flesh. Therefore, what God has joined together, no human being must separate."

Mk. 10:2-12 – "So they are no longer two but one flesh. Therefore what God has joined together, no human being must separate… Whoever divorces his wife and marries another commits adultery against her; and if she divorces her husband and marries another, she commits adultery." Jesus is quite definite on the matter.

LIFE AFTER DEATH

Some claim that souls remain in some kind of suspended animation as they await judgment at the end of time. The scriptures do not afford the evil this consolation.

Lk. 20:38 – "…He is not God of the dead, but of the living, for to him all are alive." Jesus' own words state that the dead are alive, not in some state of suspended animation.

Mk. 12:26-27 – Jesus tells us that the dead are indeed living: "As for the dead being raised, have you not read in the Book of Moses, in the passage about the bush, how God told him, 'I am the God of Abraham, [the] God of Isaac, and [the] God of Jacob'? He is not God of the dead but of the living. You are greatly misled."

Is. 14:9-10 – "The nether world below is all astir preparing for your coming; it awakens the shades to greet you, all the leaders of the earth; it has the kings of all nations rise from their thrones. All of them speak out and say to you, 'You too have become weak like us, you are the same as we.'" The scenario by which the spirits in the nether world meet the newly arrived is spelled out. Note that the spirits of the dead are responsive. They have not dissolved, nor are they deceased.

Rev. 14:9-11 – "Anyone who worships the beast or its image, or accepts its mark on forehead or hand, will also drink the wine of God's fury… The smoke of the fire that torments them will rise forever and ever, and there will be no relief day or night for those who worship the beast or its image…" If "the smoke of the fire" that torments the damned lasts "forever and ever," how is it that their torment does not?

Heb. 12:1 – "...Since we are surrounded by so great a cloud of witnesses..." Refers to the souls of the Old Testament exemplars of faith who are not dead, but live on in the spirit.

2 Pet. 2:17 – "These people are waterless springs and mists driven by a gale; for them the gloom of darkness has been reserved."

Phil. 1:23 – "I long to depart this life and be with Christ, for that is far better." St. Paul does not say, "I long to depart this life and sleep until the end of time."

Wis. 1:16 - 2:3 – The mistaken notion that the dead will not enter into eternal life, but will have their spirits dissolved into the ethers, is an ancient one. Scripture directly contradicts this error: "...they who said among themselves, thinking not aright...our body will be ashes and our spirit will be poured abroad like unresisting air..."

Eph. 3:15 – "For this reason I kneel before the Father, from whom every family in heaven and on earth is named..." Apparently families still exist after death.

Ezek. 32:18-20 – "Then from the midst of the nether world, the mighty warriors shall speak to Egypt: 'Whom do you excel in beauty? Come down, you and your allies, lie with the uncircumcised, with those slain by the sword.'" Though dead, the mighty warriors still are able to speak. They are not slumbering.

Mt. 25:46 – Hell is eternal: "And these will go off to eternal punishment..."

Lk. 16:19-31 – The story of Lazarus the beggar. Lazarus is aware of himself, his situation, and that of his brothers still on earth. He does not even seem drowsy in Jesus' account. Now, admittedly, this is just a parable. But in making his point about selfishness, pride and almsgiving, Jesus would have scarcely misled us about the nature of the afterlife.

Lk. 9:30-31 – The persons of Moses and Elijah appear during the Transfiguration of Jesus. They are neither sleeping nor dead: "And behold, two men were conversing with him, Moses and Elijah, who appeared in glory..."

Mk. 9:4 – Again, the appearance of Moses and Elijah. Both are alive and aware.

Mt. 25:41 – "Depart from me, you accursed, into the eternal fire prepared for the devil and his angels..." It is hard to imagine why the fire is eternal if there will be no souls to suffer it.

Mk. 9:48 – "...Where their worm does not die, and the fire is not quenched." Jesus himself tells us that damnation is eternal; he is referring here to the following passage from Isaiah:

48

Is. 66:24 – "They shall go out and see the corpses of the men who rebelled against me; their worm shall not die, nor their fire be extinguished; and they shall be abhorrent to all mankind." If each soul's torment does not die, how can the case be made that the soul dies, or even that it "sleeps"?

Rev. 5:8 – "Each of the elders held a harp and gold bowls filled with incense, which are the prayers of the holy ones." Those who have died in faith present the petitions of the living before the throne of God. (See the section below, *The Communion of Saints.*)

Deut. 18:10-12 – "Let there not be found among you anyone who... consults ghosts and spirits or seeks oracles from the dead." The proscription against consulting spirits assumes that the spirits are alert and aware and able to be consulted.

Eccles. 12:7 – "...And the dust returns to the earth as it once was, and the life breath returns to God who gave it." In other words, our life breath does not dissipate when our bodies die. Our souls return to God.

1 Sam. 28:12-19 – The departed spirit of Samuel appears to Saul and speaks. He tells Saul "By tomorrow you and your sons will be with me..." So we must conclude that he is not in any state of suspended animation, but alert and aware and able to "be with" others.

Heb. 12:22-23 – "...You have approached Mount Zion and the city of the living God, the heavenly Jerusalem, and countless angels in festal gathering, and the assembly of the firstborn enrolled in heaven, and God the judge of all, and the spirits of the just made perfect, and Jesus the mediator of a new covenant..."

2 Mac. 12:42-46 – "...He made atonement for the dead that they might be freed from this sin." To be freed from their sin, they must still exist.

2 Mac. 15:12-15 – When the former high priest, the "good and virtuous" Onias, was praying before the Jewish community, "...another man appeared, distinguished by his white hair and dignity, and with an air about him of extraordinary, majestic authority. Onias then said of him, 'This is God's prophet Jeremiah, who loves his brethren and fervently prays for his people and their holy city.'" The scripture tells us (v. 11) that this vision is "worthy of belief." Since the vision includes the statement that Jeremiah is active in the afterlife, both loving and praying, this passage alone refutes the doctrine of "soul sleep" that some denominations adhere to.

Heb. 9:27 – "...Human beings die once, and after this the judgment..." There is no bodily death followed by a death of the soul, as some claim. In this passage, the author is disputing that error.

Sir. 14:16 – "Give, take and treat yourself well, for in the nether world there are no joys to seek." If the dead were dissolved or unconscious, this passage would make no sense.

Rev. 21:7-8 – "The victor will inherit these gifts, and I shall be his God, and he will be my son. But as for cowards, the unfaithful, the depraved... their lot is in the burning pool of fire...""

1 Jn. 3:2 – "Beloved, we are God's children now; what we shall be has not yet been revealed." The end times are obscure.

Jer. 15:1 – "...Even if Moses and Samuel stood before me..." Apparently the possibility exists that Moses and Samuel *could* stand before God— as indeed Moses and Elijah, fully awake and aware, did stand before Jesus as they spoke to him (Lk. 9:30-31).

There are scripture passages that do appear to refer to death as sleep (Job 14:12), but they are speaking in physical terms. Our earthly bodies do appear to be asleep when we die, even as our spirits live on.

THE COMMUNION OF SAINTS

The Church believes that the perfection achieved by the faithful is not extinguished at death, but lives on in heaven, as the holy ones take their places as newly victorious members of the Mystical Body. As the documents of Vatican II state: "By the hidden and kindly mystery of God's will, a supernatural solidarity reigns among men. A consequence of this is that the sin of one person harms other people just as one person's holiness helps others. In this way, Christian believers help each other reach their supernatural destiny... This is the very ancient dogma called the communion of saints. It means that the life of each individual child of God is joined in Christ and through Christ by a wonderful link to the life of all his other Christian brethren. Together, they form the supernatural unity of Christ's Mystical Body so that, as it were, a single mystical person is formed" (Sacrosanctum Concilium 4-5).

Acts 9:1-5 – "Now Saul, still breathing murderous threats against the disciples of the Lord, went to the high priest and asked him for letters to the synagogues in Damascus, that, if he should find any men or women who belonged to the Way, he might bring them back to Jerusalem in chains. On his journey, as he was nearing Damascus, a light from the sky suddenly flashed around him. He fell to the ground and heard a voice saying to him, 'Saul, Saul, why are you persecuting me?' He said, 'Who are you, sir?' The reply came, 'I am Jesus, whom you are persecuting.'" Of course the Bible explicitly states that Saul never met Jesus on earth, and Jesus' earthly body was no longer on earth when this event took place. So in his accusation of Saul, Jesus was identifying his followers—those whom Saul *was* persecuting—with himself. By persecuting Jesus' followers, Saul was actually persecuting Jesus. Therefore, according to Jesus himself, we Christians are one with him in his Mystical Body. This is the essence of the doctrine of the Communion of Saints.

1 Cor. 12:12-27 – "But God has so constructed the body as to give greater honor to a part that is without it, so that there may be no division in the body, but that the parts may have the same concern for one another. If [one] part suffers, all the parts suffer with it; if one part is honored, all the parts share its joy." St. Paul teaches in painstaking detail the theology of the Mystical Body. His point is simple: that even if we think we are alone and do not need others, we are wrong. Salvation is not an individual matter; love can only blossom in community.

Eph. 1:22-23 – "And he put all things beneath his feet and gave him as head over all things to the church, which is his body, the fullness of the one who fills all things in every way." Again, St. Paul is quite explicit about the unity of believers in the Mystical Body of Christ. God's covenant is not forged with us as individuals, but with the entire community of believers.

Eph. 4:15-16 – "Rather, living the truth in love, we should grow in every way into him who is the head, Christ, from whom the whole body, joined and held together by every supporting ligament, with the proper functioning of each part, brings about the body's growth and builds itself up in love." Love is represented by the concern that is implicit in the Communion of Saints and is fulfilled through the ancient practice of intercessory prayer.

Rom. 12:4-8 – "For as in one body we have many parts, and all the parts do not have the same function, so we, though many, are one body in Christ and individually parts of one another." This is an excellent description of the doctrine of the Communion of Saints.

Gal. 3:28 – "There is neither Jew nor Greek, there is neither slave nor free person, there is not male and female; for you are all one in Christ Jesus." St. Paul says we are all "one"—which is what the word "communion" refers to.

Col. 1:18 – "He is the head of the body, the church." Again, St. Paul is quite explicit: The Church *is* the Body of Christ.

Rom. 8:35-39 – St. Paul tells us that not even death can separate the faithful from the love of Christ and, therefore, from one another: "What will separate us from the love of Christ? Will anguish, or distress, or persecution, or famine, or nakedness, or peril, or the sword?... No, in all these things we conquer overwhelmingly through him who loved us."

Col. 3:15 – "And let the peace of Christ control your hearts, the peace into which you were also called in one body." Having Christ as our "personal savior" is only part of the story. Our faith is more than just a personal matter. It brings us into union with the entire community of believers.

Jn. 17:11-21 – "I pray not only for them, but also for those who will believe in me through their word, so that they may all be one, as you, Father, are in me and I in you, that they also may be in us, that the world may believe that you sent me." This is Jesus' astonishing "unity prayer." Jesus is upholding the union of all believers, through all time, in the communion of saints.

1 Cor. 10:17 – The Church is one in Christ in the Eucharist: "Because the loaf of bread is one, we, though many, are one body, for we all partake of the one loaf." The Communion of Saints culminates in the Sacrament of the Eucharist. The sacrament is the source of our unity in Christ.

In 350 A.D., St. Cyril wrote a remarkable and exquisitely detailed description of the Mass, which clearly corresponds with today's Mass. In it we find this beautiful statement on the family of God which we all belong to, and which even today we pray for in every Mass: "...upon completion of the spiritual Sacrifice, the bloodless worship, over that propitiatory victim, we call upon God for the common peace of the Churches, for the welfare of the world, for kings, for soldiers and allies, for the sick, for the afflicted, and in summary, we all pray and offer this Sacrifice for all who are in need. Then we make mention also of those who have already fallen asleep: first, the patriarchs, prophets, apostles, and martyrs, that through their prayers and supplications God would receive our petition; next, we make mention also of the holy fathers and bishops who have already fallen asleep, and, to put it simply, of all among us who have already fallen asleep; for we believe that it will be of very great benefit to the souls of those for whom the petition is carried up, while this holy and most solemn Sacrifice is laid out." ('The Faith of the Early Fathers,' Vol. 1, William A. Jurgens, [Collegeville, Minnesota: Liturgical Press, 1970] p. 363.) The faithful in heaven and on earth are united in the Person of Jesus through the Sacrament of the Eucharist. This is the meaning of the Communion of Saints.

INTERCESSORY PRAYER

Intercessory prayer is an ancient tradition among the faithful. The examples of it in scripture are numerous. When we "pray to" the saints, we are merely asking one another to intercede with God, just as Abraham, Moses, Job and St. Paul interceded with God on behalf of others during their lifetimes. We are not in any way taking away from Jesus' role as King, Savior, and Mediator. Instead, we are experiencing the unity of the Mystical Body and displaying Christian care and concern for our brethren.

Job 42:8 – The three verbose friends of Job, Eliphaz, Bildad and Zophar, express dismay that God intends to punish them for their pride and their glibness. Where upon God's response is quite telling, he says, "...let my servant Job pray for you, for his prayer I will accept, not to punish you severely." Not only does God refuse to accept their pleas for forgiveness, he directs them to ask Job to intercede for them. Only when Job prays for them does God grant them his forgiveness.

1 Tim. 2:1-3 – "First of all, then, I ask that supplications, prayers, petitions and thanksgivings be offered for everyone..." We are explicitly urged by St. Paul to pray for one another.

2 Tim. 1:16-18 – "May the Lord grant him to find mercy from the Lord..." Here St. Paul is himself offering an intercessory prayer for Onesiphorus, who has died. Intercessory prayer for the dead is thus both biblical and apostolic.

2 Tim. 1:3 – "...I remember you constantly in my prayers, night and day." If all that's needed is for Timothy to pray for himself, directly to God, without any intervention from Paul, then why does Paul bother to undertake such an ambitious prayer schedule on Timothy's behalf? The answer of course is the spirit of charity, which the Communion of Saints so strongly recommends.

Mt. 5:44 – "...Pray for those who persecute you." Here Jesus himself commands us to intercede on behalf of others, including our enemies.

Rom. 10:1 – "Brothers, my heart's desire and prayer to God on their behalf is for salvation." Again, St. Paul intercedes for others in prayer.

1 Jn. 5:16 – "If anyone sees his brother sinning, if the sin is not deadly, he should pray to God and he will give him life." The apostle is urging us to pray for the sanctity of others.

Heb. 5:1 – Throughout salvation history, priests have been called upon to offer prayers and sacrifices on behalf of the community: "Every high priest is taken from among men and made their representative before God, to offer gifts and sacrifices for sins." Both intercession and expiation are explicitly referred to here.

James 5:13-16 – We are instructed to summon a priest to pray for us; we are told his prayer will be more powerful than ours: "Is anyone among you sick? He should summon the presbyters of the church, and they should pray over him and anoint [him] with oil in the name of the Lord, and the prayer of faith will save the sick person, and the Lord will raise him up... The fervent prayer of a righteous person is very powerful." James is referring to the Sacrament of Healing.

James 5:16 – "...Pray for one another, that you may be healed." St. James is directing us to offer intercessory prayer for those who are ill.

Gen. 18:23-28 – Abraham intercedes with God on behalf of Sodom, as he seeks to lower the number of just individuals required for the city to be spared: "Will you sweep away the innocent with the guilty? Suppose there were fifty innocent people in the city, would you wipe out the place, rather than spare it for the sake of the fifty innocent people within it?" And God responds positively to Abraham's intercession, acceding to his request.

Matt. 19:28 – "Amen, I say to you that you who have followed me, in the new age, when the Son of Man is seated on his throne of glory, will yourselves sit on twelve thrones, judging the twelve tribes of Israel." Jesus has graciously given mankind a role in the kingdom of God. Whether it's praying for one another, or even judging the twelve tribes of Israel, we are not detracting from or supplanting God's glory, but sharing in it.

Rev. 5:8 – "Each of the elders held a harp and gold bowls filled with incense, which are the prayers of the holy ones." Those who have gone before us in faith are clearly shown to intercede on our behalf, as they present our prayers before the throne of the living God.

Rev. 8:3-4 – "He was given a great quantity of incense to offer, along with the prayers of all the holy ones..." Our prayers on earth are offered before the throne by the holy ones in heaven. We are all united in our faith and in the sacrifice of the Lamb.

Rev. 6:9-17 – The prayers of the martyrs in heaven are responsible for God's wrath being unleashed against the earth for the spilling of their innocent blood: "They cried out in a loud voice, 'How long will it be, holy and true master, before you sit in judgment and avenge our blood on the inhabitants of the earth?'... Then the sky was divided like a torn scroll curling up, and every mountain and island was moved from its place. The kings of the earth, the nobles, the military officers, the rich, the powerful, and every slave and free person hid themselves in caves and among mountain crags. They cried out..." The prayers of the holy ones have a direct and significant effect upon the world. This is the very definition of intercessory prayer.

2 Cor. 1:11 – "...So that thanks may be given by many on our behalf for the gift granted us through the prayers of many." The power of prayer is tied to the gifts given by God to the community of the faithful.

Mt. 21:22 – "Whatever you ask for in prayer with faith you will receive." Note that Jesus does not put limitations on our prayer. Instead, "whatever" we ask for will be granted—including, we must assume, intentions we seek on another's' behalf.

Acts 12:5 – "Peter thus was being kept in prison, but prayer by the church was fervently being made to God on his behalf." This is another clear example of intercessory prayer, one in which the entire community of the faithful prays for Peter's safety.

2 Mac. 3:31 – "Soon some of the companions of Heliodorus begged Onias to invoke the Most High, praying that the life of the man who was about to expire might be spared." This is a clear case of a group of individuals engaging in intercessory prayer on behalf of a specific shared intention.

2 Mac. 12:42-46 – "Thus he made atonement for the dead that they might be freed from this sin." Clearly, intercessory prayers for the dead pre-dated Jesus' own time—by hundreds of years, in fact.

Num. 12 – Miriam rebels: "Is it through Moses alone that the Lord speaks? Does he not speak through us also?" When contracting leprosy punishes Miriam, Moses prays for God to remit Miriam's punishment. Only after Moses prays does God relent.

Gen. 48:15-16 – Jacob prays for his grandsons: "May the God in whose ways my fathers Abraham and Isaac walked...bless these boys..."

Tob. 12:12 – In heaven, the Angel Raphael presented Tobit and Sarah's prayers to God. The angel was acting as an intercessor for them: "I can now tell you that when you, Tobit, and Sarah prayed, it was I who presented and read the record of your prayer before the Glory of the Lord..."

Lev. 5:5-6 – "...Whoever is guilty in any of these cases shall confess the sin he has incurred, and as his sin offering for the sin he has committed he shall bring to the Lord a female animal from the flock, a ewe lamb or a she-goat. The priest shall then make atonement for the sin." Intercessory prayer for atonement has been part of our spiritual tradition since the beginning.

Rom. 15:30 – "I urge you, [brothers,] by our Lord Jesus Christ and by the love of the Spirit, to join me in the struggle by your prayers to God on my behalf..." St. Paul is actually asking his readers to unite themselves to his ministry through prayer. This is a beautiful way in which to regard intercessory prayer.

Zech. 1:12-13 – An angel prays for Jerusalem: "Then the angel of the Lord spoke out and said, 'O Lord of hosts, how long will you be without mercy for Jerusalem and the cities of Judah that have felt your anger these seventy years?'" The angel is interceding on Jerusalem's behalf.

James 4:3 – Our sins actually reduce the effectiveness of our prayers: "You ask but do not receive, because you ask wrongly, to spend it on your passions."

1 Pet. 3:7 – When we commit sin, God is less likely to answer our prayers: "Likewise, you husbands should live with your wives in understanding, showing honor to the weaker female sex, since we are joint heirs of the gift of life, so that your prayers may not be hindered."

Gen. 4:4-5 – God does not view all prayers equally: "The Lord looked with favor on Abel and his offering, but on Cain and his offering he did not."

Mt. 5:23-24 – Sin affects the acceptability of our sacrifice—our prayer—to the Lord: "Therefore, if you bring your gift to the altar, and there recall that your brother has anything against you, leave your gift there at the altar; go first and be reconciled with your brother, and then come and offer your gift." Jesus is telling us that the state of our soul is examined by God when he considers our prayers. Our relationships with others affect the acceptability of our prayer. That fact makes the concept of intercessory prayer easier to grasp, since it is first and foremost "relational" prayer—prayer that is offered in community.

Ps. 45:13 – In this psalm, which is a prophetic passage referring to Mary as a princess who stands at the right hand of the Messiah, we find these words: "Then the richest of the people will seek your favor with gifts." This is a clear reference to the faithful who seek Mary's intercession.

It is a historical fact that the earliest Christians prayed for the souls of the dead. In 213 A.D., Tertullian wrote: "A woman, after the death of her husband...prays for his soul and asks that he may, while waiting, find rest; and that he may share in the first resurrection. And each year, on the anniversary of his death, she offers the sacrifice." ('The Faith of the Early Church Fathers,' *Vol. 1, William A. Jurgens, [Collegeville, Minnesota: Liturgical Press, 1970] p. 158.) The objection to praying for the dead is another innovation of the Reformation. Note also Tertullian's allusion to "the sacrifice," a clear reference to the Holy Sacrifice of the Mass, which dates back to apostolic times. Finally, it is worthwhile to point out that praying for the dead clearly points to a belief in a process of cleansing that takes place after death—a "purgatory"—for there is no need to pray for souls in heaven, and no use in praying for souls in hell. Once again we see that the beliefs of the earliest Christians were thoroughly Catholic.*

INDULGENCES

In the Catechism of the Catholic Church, we find the following passage: "From the beginning the Church has honored the memory of the dead and offered prayers in suffrage for them, above all the Eucharistic sacrifice, so that, thus purified, they may attain the beatific vision of God."[Cf. Council of Lyons II (1274):DS 856]. The Catechism also contains this statement: "The Church also commends almsgiving, indulgences, and works of penance undertaken on behalf of the dead: Let us help and commemorate them. If Job's sons were purified by their father's sacrifice, why would we doubt that our offerings for the dead bring them some consolation? Let us not hesitate to help those who have died and to offer our prayers for them." [St. John Chrysostom, Hom. in 1 Cor. 41, 5:PG 61, 361; cf. Job 1:5.]

2 Sam. 12-14 – Even after David's sin is forgiven, he must undergo cleansing; his child still dies. "Nathan answered David: 'The Lord on his part has forgiven your sin: you shall not die. But since you have utterly spurned the Lord by this deed, the child born to you must surely die.'" So we see that God still disciplines David even after he forgives him. What earthly parent does not do the same? An indulgence is the remission of this residual punishment due the sinner.

Num. 12 – When Miriam rebels— "Is it through Moses alone that the Lord speaks? Does he not speak through us also?"—Moses asks God to remove her punishment of leprosy. God answers Moses' prayer, and her punishment is remitted. Moses' prayer has thus resulted in an "indulgence" for Miriam.

Mt. 16:19 – "Whatever you bind on earth will be bound in heaven; and whatever you loose on earth shall be loosed in heaven." Jesus tells St. Peter that actions taken by the Church will be respected by—and abided by—God himself.

Dan. 4:24 – Atonement is necessary: "...atone for your sins by good deeds, and for your misdeeds with kindness to the poor..." Almsgiving has always been associated with the atonement of sins.

2 Mac. 12:42-46 – "The noble Judas...took up a collection among all his soldiers, amounting to two thousand silver drachmas, which he sent to Jerusalem to provide for an expiatory sacrifice. In doing so he acted in a very excellent and noble way, inasmuch as he had the resurrection of the dead in view; for if he were not expecting the fallen to rise again, it would have been useless and foolish to pray for them in death... Thus he made atonement for the dead that they might be freed from this sin." Praying for the remission of the sins of the dead is hardly a medieval innovation. It is a very ancient practice, one that predates Christ himself by hundreds of years.

Sir. 16:11 – "For mercy and anger alike are with him who remits and forgives..."

Lk. 7:44-50 – "'Do you see this woman? When I entered your house, you did not give me water for my feet, but she has bathed them with her tears and wiped them with her hair. You did not give me a kiss, but she has not ceased kissing my feet since the time I entered. You did not anoint my head with oil, but she anointed my feet with ointment. So I tell you, her many sins have been forgiven; hence, she has shown great love. But the one to whom little is forgiven, loves little.' He said to her, 'Your sins are forgiven.' The others at table said to themselves, 'Who is this who even forgives sins?' But he said to the woman, 'Your faith has saved you; go in peace.'" The penitent woman's loving act resulted in the remission of her sins—which is the very definition of "indulgence." Jesus granted the indulgence based on his authority as Son of God, which of course is the same authority he passes on to his Church.

PURGATORY

People tend to think of purgatory as a place, but it is actually a process—one by which those of us who do not reach perfect holiness in this life are cleansed to prepare us for heaven. It is a great gift, for unless we are made perfect, scripture tells us we will have no place in heaven:

Rev. 21:27 – "...Nothing unclean will enter it (heaven)..." For those of us who are not totally perfected in this life, the doctrine of purgatory offers great hope. For until we are perfected, we cannot enter into communion with God.

1 Cor. 3:15 – "...The person will be saved, but only as through fire." Some sort of purgation takes place even as souls are being saved.

Heb. 12:14 – "Strive for peace with everyone, and for that holiness without which no one will see the Lord." Those who die without completely achieving such peace need not despair. They will be cleansed, even after death.

2 Sam. 12:13-14 – "Then David said to Nathan, 'I have sinned against the Lord.' Nathan answered David: 'The Lord on his part has forgiven your sin; you shall not die. But since you have utterly spurned the Lord by this deed, the child born to you must surely die.'" Even after David's sin is forgiven, he must undergo punishment; his child still dies.

Heb. 12:22-23 – "No, you have approached Mount Zion and the city of the living God, the heavenly Jerusalem, and countless angels in festal gathering, and the assembly of the firstborn enrolled in heaven, and God the judge of all, and the spirits of the just made perfect..." It's hard to imagine a better three-word summary of the concept of purgatory than that phrase "spirits made perfect."

Mt. 5:18-30 – Mortal sin, venial sin, purgatory, hell: "Settle with your opponent quickly while on the way to court with him. Otherwise your opponent will hand you over to the judge, and the judge will hand you over to the guard, and you will be thrown into prison. Amen, I say to you, you will not be released until you have paid the last penny."

Lk. 12:58-59 – "If you are to go with your opponent before a magistrate, make an effort to settle the matter on the way; otherwise your opponent will turn you over to the judge, and the judge hand you over to the constable, and the constable throw you into prison. I say to you, you will not be released until you have paid the last penny." Jesus tells us all accounts must be settled before salvation can be gained. This process—of paying, of learning, of cleansing—the Church calls "purgatory."

Rev. 7:13-14 – "These are the ones who have survived the time of great distress; they have washed their robes and made them white in the blood of the Lamb. For this reason they stand before God's throne and worship him day and night in his temple." The souls who have survived the time of great distress—their trial on earth—wash their robes in the blood of the Lamb, and as a result are able to enter heaven. The cause-and-effect is quite clear. "They have washed..." and "for this reason, they stand before God's throne." The doctrine of purgatory is unmistakable.

1 Jn. 5:16-17 – "If anyone sees his brother sinning, if the sin is not deadly, he should pray to God and he will give him life. This is only for those whose sin is not deadly. There is such a thing as deadly sin, about which I do not say that you should pray. All wrongdoing is sin, but there is sin that is not deadly." When we die in sin, but the sin is not deadly, where do we go? What happens to us? We know we do not gain immediate entry into heaven, since nothing unclean can enter there (Rev. 21:27). And certainly not to hell, since John tells us the sin is not deadly. We must therefore undergo some kind of cleansing, or purgation.

Mk. 9:49 – Jesus describes purgatory: "Everyone will be salted with fire."

1 Pet. 3:19 – "...He also went to preach to the spirits in prison..." Where is this "prison"? Not heaven, certainly. But neither can it be hell.

Eph. 4:8-10 – "...He also descended into the lower [regions] of the earth..."

Mt. 12:32 – "...Whoever speaks against the Holy Spirit will not be forgiven in this age or the age to come." Here Jesus clearly implies that expiation can occur after death. Apparently some sins *are* forgiven in "the age to come."

2 Mac. 12:42-46 – "The noble Judas…took up a collection among all his soldiers, amounting to two thousand silver drachmas, which he sent to Jerusalem to provide for an expiatory sacrifice. In doing so he acted in a very excellent and noble way, inasmuch as he had the resurrection of the dead in view... Thus he made atonement for the dead that they might be freed from this sin." Judas could not have been praying for the dead if they were in hell, since prayer would not have benefited them. And if they were in heaven, prayer would not have been necessary.

The belief in purgatory is not, as some claim, a medieval "innovation." Quite the contrary. This doctrine actually dates back farther in Church history than both the doctrine of the Holy Trinity and the canon of the New Testament. Around 210 A.D., we find Tertullian stating: "...if we understand that prison of which the Gospel speaks to be Hades, and if we interpret the last farthing (Mt. 5:25-26) to be the light offense which is to be expiated there before the resurrection, no one will doubt that the soul undergoes some punishments in Hades, without prejudice to the fullness of the resurrection, after which recompense will be made through the flesh also." (The Faith of the Early Fathers, Vol. 1, William A. Jurgens, [Collegeville, Minnesota: Liturgical Press, 1970] p. 145.)

THE SACRAMENT OF RECONCILIATION

The act of confessing our sins requires us to acknowledge them as our own. It serves to humble us. We are forced to look our faults full in the face and contemplate the devastating toll our own failings take on the lives of others. By divesting us of our pet illusions and our pestilent vainglory, the act of confessing prepares us for the free gift of God's forgiveness—reconciliation—that permits the restoration and renewal of God's life within us through the sacrament. This sacrament is a great and very precious gift. No one who regularly comes to the Sacrament of Reconciliation remains mired for long in the same patterns of sinful and destructive behavior. And those who do not come to it are often unable to escape those patterns. Even the 12-Step programs recognize the need for us to acknowledge—and ask forgiveness for—our destructive behaviors before we can hope to break out of them. Through the grace and mercy of God, the Sacrament of Reconciliation gives us power over sin. Indeed, it can actually transform our sins into glorious conduits of God's grace in a way that only someone who has experienced the gift of the sacrament can explain. Through Reconciliation, all our tears are wiped away, and death gives way to new life.

Mt. 18:18 – "Amen, I say to you, whatever you bind on earth shall be bound in heaven, and whatever you loose on earth shall be loosed in heaven." This authority, which Jesus passes on to his apostles, is clear. Thus, when others claim "only God can forgive sins," we can agree without question, pointing out that he does so through the authority given by Jesus to his Church.

Mt. 16:19 – "Whatever you bind on earth will be bound in heaven; and whatever you loose on earth shall be loosed in heaven." Again, Jesus' intention—and the authority he passes on to his followers—could not be clearer. Does God forgive sins? Absolutely. But he does not deny this salvific act—the forgiveness of sins—to his Mystical Body on earth.

Jn. 20:23 – "Whose sins you forgive are forgiven them, and whose sins you retain are retained." Again, this is an explicit bestowal of the authority to forgive sins from Jesus to his apostles. Those who deny the usefulness of this sacrament stand in opposition to the scriptures that, as we see, affirm it again and again. Those who ask why we need men to forgive sins should direct their question to Jesus, who clearly desired his followers to forgive sins.

2 Cor. 5:18 – The Sacrament of Reconciliation dates to apostolic times: "And all this is from God, who has reconciled us to himself through Christ and given us the ministry of reconciliation." St. Paul could hardly be more specific.

2 Cor. 2:10 – "Whomever you forgive anything, so do I. For indeed what I have forgiven, if I have forgiven anything, has been for you in the presence of Christ..." Clearly, whenever St. Paul forgave sins, it was truly Christ who forgave them. Paul is giving us, in a nutshell, the theology of the Sacrament of Reconciliation. St. Paul is telling us that when he forgave sins he was acting—as the priest acts today—*in persona Christi*, "in the person of Christ." Again, what could be clearer?

Acts 19:18 – "Many of those who had become believers came forward and openly acknowledged their former practices." The confessing of sins has been part of the life of the faithful from the beginnings of our faith.

James 5:15-16 – "Therefore, confess your sins to one another and pray for one another, that you may be healed." Confession, which requires repentance, plays an integral part in God's gift of forgiveness.

1 Jn. 1:9 – "If we acknowledge our sins, he is faithful and just and will forgive our sins and cleanse us from every wrongdoing." Note the condition under which St. John tells us God will forgive us—that we "acknowledge our sins." We are not forgiven in advance of any and all sins we might ever commit—regardless of whether we repent—as some Protestant traditions claim.

Mk. 2:7 – The scribes object to Jesus' forgiveness of sins: "Why does this man speak that way? He is blaspheming. Who but God alone can forgive sins?" Protestants who object to the Sacrament of Reconciliation— "Why do you need a man to forgive sins? Only God can do that!"—are in agreement with these scribes who were pitted against our Lord.

Mt. 9:2-8 – "When Jesus saw their faith, he said to the paralytic, 'Courage, child, your sins are forgiven.' At that, some of the scribes said to themselves, 'This man is blaspheming.'" Again, those who object to the sacrament are in agreement with the scribes, not the followers of Jesus. The fact is, we humans possess bodies and we live in time, so it makes sense for God to have given us a tangible experience—an assurance that exists in time and space—of forgiveness.

Lev. 5:5-6 – "...Whoever is guilty in any of these cases shall confess the sin he has incurred, and as his sin offering for the sin he has committed he shall bring to the Lord a female animal from the flock, a ewe lamb or a she-goat. The priest shall then make atonement for the sin." Confession, sacrifice and atonement have been a part of our faith tradition since the beginning. The point is repeated in Lev. 19:20-22.

The Sacrament of Reconciliation was practiced by the ancient Christians. We find a marvelous explanation, both sacramental and psychological, in one of Origen's homilies, dating back to about 245 A.D., some 150 years before the canon of the New Testament: "There is something wonderful hidden in this, whereby confession of sins is commanded. For they are to be confessed, whatever kind they be; and all that we do must be brought forward in public. Whatever we have done in secret, whatever sin we have committed by word alone or even in our secret thoughts—all must be made public, all must be brought forward. It will indeed be brought forward by him who is both the accuser of sin and the instigator thereof. For that one who now incites us to sin is the very one who will accuse us when we have sinned. If, therefore, we anticipate him in life, and become the accusers of ourselves, we escape the malice of the devil, our enemy and accuser... You see, then, that confession of sin merits the remission of sin." (The Faith of the Early Fathers, Vol. 1, William A. Jurgens, [Collegeville, Minnesota: Liturgical Press, 1970] p. 207-208.)

MORTAL/VENIAL SIN

Some Protestant traditions teach that there are no degrees of sin— "Sin is sin." While all sin is undeniably evil, the Bible reveals that there are at least two distinct levels of sin: That which is deadly and that which is not. The Church calls deadly sin "mortal" and non-deadly sin "venial."

1 Jn. 5:16-17 – "If anyone sees his brother sinning, if the sin is not deadly, he should pray to God and he will give him life. This is only for those whose sin is not deadly. There is such a thing as deadly sin, about which I do not say that you should pray. All wrongdoing is sin, but there is sin that is not deadly."

Jn. 19:11 – "For this reason the one who handed me over to you had the greater sin." Jesus himself tells us there are degrees of sin.

1 Cor. 6:9-11 – "Do you not know that the unjust will not inherit the kingdom of God? Do not be deceived; neither fornicators nor idolaters..." St. Paul specifies a number of sins that are deadly—i.e., that cut us off from the life of God. If all sins were considered equal in the eyes of God, then for him to do so would have been meaningless as well as misleading.

INFANT BAPTISM

It is true that the Bible nowhere states explicitly that infants were baptized. But neither does it say they were not. As we see in Col. 2:11-12, below, circumcision was a "type"—an Old Testament precursor—of Baptism. In Jewish law, infants were circumcised at eight days. It is impossible to conceive that the New Testament fulfillment would ever be less effective, or more restrictive in its application, than the Old Testament type.

Gen. 17:12 – "Throughout the ages, every male among you, when he is eight days old, shall be circumcised…" Consent does not alter the fact that all belong to God. The child is a privileged member of God's holy nation. The idea that an individual might opt out of such a remarkable blessing could not have even occurred to the Israelites.

Ex. 13:13-14 – "Every first-born son you must redeem. If your son should ask you later on, 'What does this mean?' you should tell him…" The fact that the child is not cognizant does not eliminate the dedication of the first-born. God's claim on the first-born is absolute—regardless of whether they realize it or not. Is God's claim on the rest of us, after Jesus' redemptive sacrifice, less strong or less valid today? On the contrary, it is stronger.

Acts 2:38-39 – "Peter [said] to them, 'Repent and be baptized, every one of you, in the name of Jesus Christ for the forgiveness of your sins; and you will receive the gift of the Holy Spirit.'" This is the primary text many Protestants cite in upholding their position against infant Baptism. They feel St. Peter was speaking doctrinally, stating that repentance is required before Baptism can be administered. And of course we all agree that infants cannot repent. But notice the very next verse of Peter's sermon: "For the promise is made to you and to your children and to all those far off, whomever the Lord God will call." Clearly, the promise of Baptism—which is salvation—does not exclude children; indeed, here St. Peter expressly extends it to them. Note too that the phrase, "your children," shows beyond question that St. Peter was not addressing the infants or the children in attendance, but the adults. And adults *are* required to repent of their sins when they are converted to Christ and baptized. Of course infants, who have not sinned, have no need to repent. Instead, they are welcomed into the community, and the evil one's claim on them—which results from the sin of Adam, or "original sin"—is washed away in the purifying waters of the sacrament. (See the next section, *The Saving Nature of Baptism.*)

2 Thess. 3:10 – "…When we were with you, we instructed you that if anyone was unwilling to work, neither should that one eat." If we interpret St. Peter's directive to repent before Baptism as applying to infants (the reference here is to Acts 2:38, above), then we must apply this command of St. Paul's to them as well. For Paul—like Peter—does not specifically exclude them. Of course requiring infants to work before they are allowed to eat would mean they would starve to death, since babies are as incapable of work as they are of repentance. Yet there is absolutely no logical–or textual– basis on which to exclude them from one admonition and not the other.

64

Col. 2:11-12 – "In him you were also circumcised with a circumcision not administered by hand, by stripping of the carnal body, with the circumcision of Christ." Baptism is the fulfillment of circumcision. Babies were circumcised at the age of eight days. How is it possible the New Testament fulfillment, Baptism, would be less saving—and apply less widely—than the Old Testament precursor?

Acts 16:15 – "After she and her household had been baptized..." In the Bible, there is no mention of any exceptions being made when an entire "household" is baptized, nor will you find reference to any supposed age of consent. Also, remember that the word, "household," is even more inclusive than "family," since "household" includes slaves and servants.

Acts 16:33 – "He and all his family were baptized..." Again, no exceptions are mentioned. How likely is it that both of these family households (in this verse and the one cited above) included no young children?

Lk. 18:15-17 – "People were bringing even infants to him that he might touch them, and when the disciples saw this, they rebuked them. Jesus, however, called the children to himself and said, 'Let the children come to me and do not prevent them; for the kingdom of God belongs to such as these.'" Jesus is telling us that infants are precisely the type of people—ones with true and simple hearts—who can receive the kingdom of God. When we bar infants from Baptism, we are denying Jesus' own explicit directions to let the children—in the words of scripture, "even infants"—come to him. How can the kingdom of God belong to "even infants" if they are not permitted Baptism? Clearly it cannot, according to Jn. 3:5, where Jesus tells us: "...no one can enter the kingdom of God without being born of water and Spirit." The birth of water and Spirit is a clear reference to Baptism.

Lk. 1:15 – "...For he will be great in the sight of [the] Lord. He will drink neither wine nor strong drink. He will be filled with the Holy Spirit even from his mother's womb..." If no one can receive the Holy Spirit without repentance—as Protestants are claiming when they deny Baptism to infants—then we must conclude that infants are able to repent even in utero, since in this passage we see that St. John the Baptist was filled with the Holy Spirit even before his birth. Which means there *is* no reason to deny infants the Sacrament of Baptism.

Mt. 21:15-16 – "When the chief priests and the scribes saw the wondrous things he was doing, and the children crying out in the temple area, 'Hosanna to the Son of David,' they were indignant and said to him,

'Do you hear what they are saying?' Jesus said to them, 'Yes; and have you never read the text, 'Out of the mouths of infants and nurslings you have brought forth praise'?"

The Church has baptized infants from its earliest days. We have the testimony of a number of the early Christian leaders on this point, including Origen, who wrote in the year 244 A.D.: "The Church received from the apostles the tradition of giving Baptism even to infants." (The Faith of the Early Fathers,' Vol. 1, William A. Jurgens, [Collegeville, Minnesota: Liturgical Press, 1970] p. 209). *If, as some Protestants claim, baptizing infants is "unbiblical," then so is* not *baptizing infants. For nowhere in scripture will you find a passage forbidding the Baptism of infants. And, just as interesting, nowhere in the Bible do we find any reference whatsoever to the supposed "age of consent" which so many Protestant traditions adhere to in baptizing adolescents. As is so often the case, "sola scriptura" is less than totally conclusive. We need Sacred Tradition, passed on from one generation to the next, to recall for us the practices of the apostles. Indeed, which generation could have possibly lost track of whether or not infants were baptized in their midst in years past? Under what circumstances could such worship practices and traditions be lost to the entire community? Such a thing defies logic.*

THE SAVING NATURE OF BAPTISM

Despite the fact that many Protestant denominations baptize—most using the Trinitarian formula prescribed in Mt. 28:19 (below)—many do not acknowledge the clear biblical teaching that Baptism is regenerative. If they did, they would be violating one of their most basic doctrines, "sola fide," or salvation by "faith alone." Yet the Bible is crystal-clear: Baptism is no mere symbol; it is sacrament, which means it is both a symbol and a grace-filled reality. Baptism saves. And where Protestant theology posits a dichotomy between faith and Baptism, the ancient Catholic tradition views them as inseparable.

Ezek. 36:25 – "I will sprinkle clean water upon you to cleanse you from all your impurities, and from all your idols I will cleanse you." No mention is made of any merely symbolic purification here. The sprinkling—Baptism—is the cleansing agent promised by God in the Old Testament. It is nothing short of cause and effect. Note also that the form of Baptism prophesied is not total immersion, but sprinkling.

1 Pet. 3:18-21 – "…God patiently waited in the days of Noah, during the building of the ark, in which a few persons, eight in all, were saved, through water. This prefigured baptism, which saves you now."

St. Peter is telling us that Baptism saves us now as surely as the flood cleansed the world of sin in the days of Noah. The flood was not just symbolic; how can anyone claim Baptism is? And note that Peter is absolutely explicit about Baptism's saving effect: "…baptism, which saves you now." Peter's statement is simple and clear: Baptism saves.

Zech. 13:1 – "On that day there shall be open to the house of David and to the inhabitants of Jerusalem, a fountain to purify from sin and uncleanness." The text says nothing about a merely symbolic cleansing. This allusion is to the fountain of Jesus Christ, who provides for us the saving waters of Baptism. As Christ is our real and efficacious Savior, so too is the Baptism he instituted for us real and efficacious.

Mt. 3:16-17 – "After Jesus was baptized, he came up from the water and behold, the heavens were opened [for him], and he saw the Spirit of God descending like a dove [and] coming upon him. And a voice came from the heavens, saying, 'This is my beloved Son, with whom I am well pleased.'" The Bible tells us that it is Jesus' Baptism that causes the Spirit of God to descend upon him. And this is no mere symbolic event, since it is the reality of the Holy Spirit that is present, and it is the Father's actual voice—with real sound—that manifests itself from the heavens. At this moment in time beside the Jordan River, heaven comes to earth—in a real, physical sense, in time and in space, and not merely symbolically. The same thing happens to us when we are baptized. This is the rebirth in "water and Spirit," which Jesus says we must undergo to be saved. Now, as then, it is an actual bestowal of the Trinity—Father, Son and Holy Spirit.

Jn. 3:5 – "Amen, Amen, I say to you, no one can enter the kingdom of God without being born of water and Spirit." Baptism is the only possible meaning here. The phrase "water and Spirit" refers to the sacramental aspect of Baptism; it is both physical symbol and spiritual reality. And Jesus tells us that we cannot enter the kingdom without being "born again," or baptized. So when you are asked whether you have been "born again" by an evangelizing Protestant, assure him that on the day of your Baptism you were indeed "born again"—of water and the Spirit, as noted by the Lord himself. One more interesting point: This passage takes place as part of a conversation between Jesus and Nicodemus. Immediately after it, we see Jesus going out to baptize—the one and only time the scriptures tell us he does so: "After this, Jesus and his disciples went into the region of Judea, where he spent some time with them baptizing" (v. 22). Coincidence? There are no coincidences in scripture.

Jn. 1:33 – "I did not know him, but the one who sent me to baptize with water told me, 'On whomever you see the Spirit come down and remain, he is the one who will baptize with the Holy Spirit.'" If the Baptism of Christ were water functioning as a mere symbol, then how could John refer to it as a Baptism of the Holy Spirit? In the scriptures, the Holy Spirit is shown to be an agent—and not just a symbol—of change. Thus, in a real sense, denying the regenerative power of Baptism is to deny the doctrine of the Holy Trinity.

Acts 2:38-41 – "Peter [said] to them, 'Repent and be baptized, every one of you, in the name of Jesus Christ for the forgiveness of your sins; and you will receive the gift of the Holy Spirit.'" St. Peter says nothing of symbols. Rather, he explicitly states that Baptism results in the forgiveness of sins and the imparting of the Holy Spirit.

Acts 22:16 – "Now, why delay? Get up and have yourself baptized and your sins washed away, calling upon his name." The prominent Christian Ananias is telling the Pharisee Paul how to respond to God's call. He is explicit about the saving effect of the sacrament: it results in the forgiveness of sins. From the earliest times, it is clear; the Church has held that Baptism results in a real cleansing from sin, and the incorporation of the individual into the Mystical Body of Christ. It was not until the Reformation—some 1500 years later—that innovations arose in the form of false dichotomies (faith vs. works; faith vs. law; faith vs. Baptism, etc.), and Baptism was thereafter viewed by some as a mere symbol of faith.

Gal. 3:27 – "For all of you who were baptized into Christ have clothed yourselves with Christ." Note that St. Paul did not write "all of you who *believe* in Christ." Baptism has a definite effect.

Tit. 3:4-7 – "But when the kindness and generous love of God our savior appeared, not because of any righteous deeds we had done but because of his mercy, he saved us through the bath of rebirth and renewal by the Holy Spirit, whom he richly poured out on us through Jesus Christ our savior... ." St. Paul's reference to "the bath of rebirth"—or, as it's rendered in other translations, "the washing of regeneration"—is quite explicit. That is precisely what the Catholic Church teaches that Baptism is, a rebirth in water and the Spirit. Of St. Paul's many references to Baptism—or to washing and rebirth—there is never even a hint that he is speaking of symbols only. Never, for example, does he say, "a washing that *symbolizes* rebirth," although he certainly could have. Also, note the definite article "the" which precedes the word "bath." This restricts our focus to a specific act of washing which cannot be anything but Baptism.

Mt. 28:19 – "Go therefore, and make disciples of all nations, baptizing them in the name of the Father, and of the Son, and of the holy Spirit..." Jesus' directive is no mere suggestion or proposal. It is unequivocal—cause and effect. Baptism results in discipleship. Through Baptism we become adopted brothers of Christ, and members of his Mystical Body on earth, the Church.

The Early Fathers, in text after text, generation after generation, repeatedly uphold the regenerative nature of Baptism. The idea that the sacrament is merely symbolic is simply not found in Christian literature until the 16th century, when certain of the followers of the Reformers, intent on distancing themselves from the Catholic Church, developed this innovative teaching from a broad interpretation of a limited number of biblical verses. Yet even those verses don't reference Baptism at all, but faith, because the only way one can uphold the Protestant position that Baptism is merely symbolic is to drive a wedge between Baptism and faith. But in the historic Church, faith and Baptism were viewed, not as separate at all, but as integrally related. The fact is, one sees not even a hint in the scriptures that Baptism is anything less than fully regenerative and salvific.

THE MASS

For two thousand years, dating back to the times of the apostles, the Holy Sacrifice of the Mass has been the central act of Christian worship. It is the celebration of the new Passover, complete with the unblemished Lamb whose Blood was shed and whose Flesh is to be consumed for the salvation of mankind.

Acts 2:42 – "They devoted themselves to the teachings of the apostles and to the communal life, to the breaking of the bread and to the prayers." The earliest believers referred to the Eucharist as "the breaking of the bread." We see that the Mass was celebrated even in apostolic times.

Acts 20:7 – "On the first day of the week when we gathered to break bread, Paul spoke to them..." This is a clear reference to Sunday Mass being celebrated by the faithful in apostolic times.

Mk. 14:22 – "While they were eating, he took bread, said the blessing, broke it, and gave it to them, and said, 'Take it; this is my body.' Then he took a cup, gave thanks, and gave it to them, and they all drank from it. He said to them, 'This is my blood of the covenant, which will be shed for many.'" The first Eucharist was celebrated by Jesus at the Last Supper. A priest speaks these same words today, whenever Mass is said.

Lk. 22:14-20 – "...He took the bread, said the blessing, broke it, and gave it to them, saying, 'This is my body, which will be given for you;

do this in memory of me.'" Again, these are the words spoken today by the celebrant at every Mass.

1 Cor. 5:7-8 – "For our paschal lamb, Christ, has been sacrificed. Therefore, let us celebrate the feast..." Here St. Paul is referring to the Mass, the new Passover, where the people of God, united with the perfect sacrifice of Jesus through his Body and Blood in the Eucharist, pass over from sin and death into the new life of salvation. Catholics regularly refer to the Mass with all these terms used by Paul: Sacrifice, celebration and feast.

Zech. 14:21 – "And every pot in Jerusalem and in Judah shall be holy to the Lord of hosts; and all who come to sacrifice shall take them and cook in them." This extended eschatological passage in Zechariah, beginning with 14:1, describes "the day of the Lord." It may be interpreted variously as either the end times, or the time after the arrival of the Messiah. Either way, the ongoing sacrifice by the faithful ones is presaged in the verse quoted above. Thus, the once-for-all sacrifice did not cease on the first Good Friday, but continues. Also note the association between the sacrifice and a meal. The Eucharist is clearly prophesied here.

Mal. 1:11 – "For from the rising of the sun, even to its setting, my name is great among the nations; and everywhere they bring sacrifice to my name, and a pure offering." Is this a reference to the sacrifices made under the old covenant—lambs, cattle and doves? No, for St. Paul tells us those were of no avail—i.e., they were not pure. Also, "the nations" did not take part in the sacrifices of the Israelites. So we must conclude that this is a reference to the Holy Sacrifice of the Mass, offered through the ongoing and eternal priesthood of Jesus.

Rev. 5:6 – "Then I saw standing in the midst of the throne and the four living creatures and the elders a Lamb that seemed to have been slain." John's vision of heaven includes Jesus' sacrifice, which is eternal and ongoing. Thus, the Mass is the form of heavenly worship that is eternally offered before the throne of the Father. With its vestments and censors, prayers of petition and thanksgiving; its messages of encouragement and admonition; the Presence of the Lamb who was sacrificed; the prostration, adoration and endlessly repeated prayers, the activity described in Revelation is undeniably both a liturgical celebration and a sacrifice—in other words, a Mass. This topic is dealt with in detail in Scott Hahn's book, *The Lamb's Supper: The Mass as Heaven on Earth*, which is mentioned in the bibliography that concludes this book.

Heb. 13:8 – "Jesus Christ is the same yesterday, today and forever." This is why his sacrifice can be presented for all ages on earth in the Mass, just as it is presented for all eternity in Paradise (see passage immediately above).

Jude 12 – Jude refers to the celebration of the Mass as a "love feast"; he also warns against any desecration of the sacrament: "These are blemishes on your love feasts, as they carouse fearlessly and look after themselves." The earliest community of believers gathered to celebrate a feast, a sacrifice, a meal—all terms in use even today to refer to the Mass.

In his "Catechetical Lectures," which date to around 350 A.D., St. Cyril of Jerusalem gives a marvelous description of the Mass as it existed in his time, as well as an account of the sacraments that are received by those newly accepted into the Church. Many of the prayers and responses are nearly identical to those used today, and of course the Real Presence of Christ in the Eucharist is described in great detail: "Let us, then, with full confidence, partake of the Body and Blood of Christ. For in the figure of bread His Body is given to you, and in the figure of wine His Blood is given to you, so that by partaking of the Body and Blood of Christ, you might become united in body and blood with Him. For thus do we become Christ-bearers, His Body and Blood being distributed through our members. And thus it is that we become, according to the blessed Peter, sharers of the divine nature." ('The Faith of the Early Fathers,' Vol. 1, William A. Jurgens, [Collegeville, Minnesota: Liturgical Press, 1970] pp. 360-61.) Keep in mind that St. Cyril was writing 50 years prior to the promulgation of the canon of the scriptures. So we see that the Mass and the sacraments are older than the Bible itself.

HOLY EUCHARIST

Jesus is clearer and more explicit concerning his real and living Presence in the Eucharist than he is on any other teaching. He is most insistent upon it, in fact.

Jn. 6:22-71 – "Amen, amen, I say to you, unless you eat the flesh of the Son of Man and drink his blood, you do not have life within you. Whoever eats my flesh and drinks my blood has eternal life, and I will raise him on the last day. For my flesh is true food, and my blood is true drink." When many questioned this "hard teaching" and turned away, Jesus did not call them back or correct any misunderstanding they might have had. For there was none. Instead, he insisted that he meant what he said, even if it might mean losing his beloved apostles: "Since Jesus knew that his disciples were murmuring about this, he said to them,

'Does this shock you? What if you were to see the Son of Man ascending to where he was before?... The words I have spoken are spirit and life. But there are some of you who do not believe...' Jesus then said to the Twelve, 'Do you also want to leave?' Simon Peter answered him, 'Master, to whom shall we go? You have the words of eternal life.'" Like Peter, we are called to believe, even when we do not understand. The question of symbolism vs. Real Presence is dealt with summarily in Jesus' words, "...my flesh is true food, and my blood is true drink." "True" as opposed to merely "symbolic." The difficulty the disciples had in grasping these teaching stems from the fact that this is *not* another parable to be "explained" like the sower and the seed. The Eucharist *is* Jesus' Body and Blood, just as he says (see also the passage below). It would *not* have been difficult for his followers to grasp this teaching had Jesus been speaking only in parables or metaphors—if, for example, the "true food" were really just Jesus' words, as many Protestants claim. There would have been no need for the confused disciples to leave. Author and apologist Carl Olson makes these additional points: "As the passage progresses, the word which Jesus uses for 'eat' actually changes in the Greek from *phago*, which is a rather ordinary word for 'eat,' to *trogo*, which means 'to gnaw or chew.' Even *Vine's Expository Dictionary* (a Protestant reference guide), which holds to the metaphorical view of John 6, remarks: 'In John 6, the change in the Lord's use from the verb *phago* to the stronger verb *trogo* is noticeable' (p. 192). The word is never used symbolically in either the Bible or in other ancient literature. In addition, when the term 'eat my flesh' is used metaphorically in the Bible, it means, 'revile me' or 'destroy me' (see Ps. 27:2; Micah 3:1-4; Is. 9:18-20, Rev. 17:6, etc.). So if Christ were trying to convey a metaphor, he not only made a poor choice, he created a lot of confusion by essentially uttering nonsense." One final observation: It is evident that John is connecting Judas' betrayal with a lack of faith in the Eucharist (Jn. 6:70-71). One could argue that his rejection of Jesus' "hard teaching" was what ultimately led Judas to decide to hand Jesus over to the temple authorities. Note also that Judas' betrayal took place immediately after the Last Supper, in which Jesus first gave his followers his Body to eat and Blood to drink (see passage below). Judas' lack of faith in the Eucharist might well have been the very trigger that caused him to act. At the very least, the association is clear.

Mk. 14:22-24 – "While they were eating, he took bread, said the blessing, broke it, and gave it to them, and said, 'Take it; this is my body.' Then he took a cup, gave thanks, and gave it to them, and they all drank from it. He said to them, 'This is my blood of the covenant which will be shed for many.'" Jesus did not choose his words carelessly. He is referring to Ex. 24:4-8, where we see Moses ratifying the old covenant with the blood of peace offerings: "Then he took the blood and sprinkled it on the people, saying, 'This is the blood of the covenant which the Lord has made with you in accordance with all these words of his.'" Was the original covenant symbolic only? Hardly, for when the Israelites broke it, they paid a very real price: a covenantal curse. Also, note that here Jesus does not say that the contents of the cup *symbolize* the blood of the covenant which will be shed. Rather, he says the contents *are* the blood of the covenant which will be shed. We know that the "shedding" that Jesus was speaking of would prove to be all too real—not merely symbolic. So how can we assume that the "blood" that would be shed is less real than the shedding? The facts are undeniable: There is not a single verse in scripture where Jesus, the evangelists, or the apostles refer to the Eucharist as merely symbolic.

Lk. 24:13-35 – After Jesus' resurrection, two disciples spent time in deep conversation with the Lord on their way to Emmaus. They did not recognize him, even though he was teaching them from the scriptures the passages that referred to him and his passion. However, that night, over their meal, "he was made known to them in the breaking of the bread." This is a telling fact. Although the Lord was obscured to them in the scriptures—apparently "sola scriptura" was not enough for them to grasp even the Truth that was walking beside them—he was finally revealed in the Eucharistic meal. "The breaking of the bread" is a reference to an action that still takes place in the Holy Sacrifice of the Mass today, when the priest breaks the consecrated Host to re-present the broken Body of our Lord, Christ Jesus.

1 Cor. 5:7-8 – "For our paschal lamb, Christ has been sacrificed. Therefore, let us celebrate the feast…" Paul is referring to the Mass, the new Passover, where the people of God, united with the perfect sacrifice of Jesus through his Body and Blood in the Eucharist, pass over from sin and death into the new life of salvation. The Church teaches that the Mass is both sacrifice and meal.

1 Cor. 11:26-30 – "…Whoever eats the bread or drinks the cup unworthily will have to answer for the body and blood of the Lord." Here St. Paul reinforces the teaching of the Real Presence of Christ in the Eucharist. Being adjudged guilty of someone's "body and blood" is a clear reference to murder. How could anyone be guilty of murder for violating a mere symbol? This is also a key passage that affirms the Church's practice of denying the Eucharist to those who are not in full communion with the Catholic Church. St. Paul is warning us that to receive the sacrament without an accompanying faith would be an offense of the most serious nature, akin to the murder of the Lord.

Heb. 13:10-16 – "We have an altar from which those who serve the tabernacle have no right to eat." The author is differentiating between the Christian community and the Jewish people. He is saying those who continue to worship in the Jewish tradition cannot share in the Eucharistic meal. Again, this passage affirms the Catholic Church's tradition that those who are not members of the community may not share in the sacrament.

1 Cor. 10:14-17 – "The cup of blessing that we bless, is it not a participation in the blood of Christ? The bread that we break, is it not a participation in the body of Christ? Because the loaf of bread is one, we, though many, are one body, for we all partake of the one loaf." Note the word "participation." That is an active word that refers to active exchanges between people, not symbols. St. Paul could have just as easily written, "is it not a symbol of the body of Christ," but he did not. We do in fact *participate* in the Body and Blood of Christ, we don't just honor it or think of it.

Gen. 14:18 – "Melchizedek brought out bread and wine..." This mysterious high priest and king is a clear precursor to Christ—our High Priest and King. Catholic scripture scholar, Scott Hahn, notes the importance of Melchizedek in his book, *The Lamb's Supper*. Hahn observes that the roles of priest and king are only rarely united in one individual in scripture as they are in both Melchizedek and Jesus. Melchizedek's priesthood pre-dates the Levitical priesthood, so it is very ancient. Melchizedek is in fact the first high priest mentioned in scripture. Scripture tells us that Melchizedek was king of Salem—the same place where Jeru-salem—meaning "city of peace" (Ps. 76:2)—would later be built. Abraham revisited Salem years later, when he took his son Isaac up to Mount Moriah to offer him as a sacrifice to God (Gen. 22:2). Israelite tradition, as cited in 2 Chron. 3:1, associates Mount Moriah with the future site of the temple of Jerusalem. So we see that the spot where Melchizedek offered bread and wine on behalf of Abraham could well have been the very same place that Abraham later went to offer his son as sacrifice to God, and it could have been the same spot from which the Hebrew people offered their sacrifices centuries thereafter. And it could also have been the same place our High Priest,

Jesus, offered his sacrifice on Calvary. If true, this would be an astonishing geographical convergence. On another topic, it is important to note that Ps. 110 says of the coming Messiah, "Like Melchizedek you are a priest forever." This verse clearly establishes the Last Supper as a sacrifice, since it is the only time in scripture we see Jesus offering bread and wine. Since the psalm refers to Jesus as a priest "like Melchizedek," then the Last Supper meal must have also been a sacrifice—which implies both a priest and a victim. This observation reaffirms the Catholic teaching that the Last Supper was in fact the first Mass.

Belief in the Real Presence of Jesus in the Eucharist dates back to apostolic times. It is evidenced in the writings of the earliest Church fathers—among them, St. Ignatius of Antioch, who, writing in 110 A.D., states: "Take care, then, to use one Eucharist, so that whatever you do, you do according to God: for there is one Flesh of our Lord Jesus, and one cup in the union of His Blood..." ('The Faith of the Early Fathers,'Vol. 1, William A. Jurgens,[Collegeville, Minnesota: Liturgical Press, 1970] p. 22.) *Historians agree that Ignatius knew the apostles John and Peter, and was probably ordained by one of them. It is hardly likely that such a great martyr as St. Ignatius would have gone to his death to maintain the purity of the faith, declining to offer even a few grains of incense to Caesar when doing so would have saved him from the lions, yet at the same time would have ignored what he learned from the mouths of the apostles, thus corrupting the faith by propounding novel and absurd notions. This is not just unlikely, it is unthinkable. And when you add to it the fact that all the Church leaders at the time must have simultaneously traveled the same strange path to apostasy, the illogic of the "Great Apostasy" theory comes clear. Thus, the teaching of the Real Presence had to have come from the apostles, who were present at the Last Supper, and who heard Jesus preaching to the multitudes along the shores of the Galilee. The complete unanimity of the early Church fathers on this teaching allows for no other conclusion. It is also interesting to note that not a single Christian voice was raised to question this teaching for nearly fifteen hundred years.*

JESUS' "ONCE - FOR - ALL" SACRIFICE

Many Protestants believe that, in the Mass, Catholics are "re-sacrificing" Jesus and denying the "once-for-all" saving power of the Crucifixion. They state that when Jesus said, "It is finished" (Jn. 19:30) from the cross, he was speaking of his perfect sacrifice, and our redemption. However, St. Paul tells us that our salvation is completed only by the resurrection: "...if Christ has not been raised, your faith is in vain; you are still in your sins" (1 Cor. 15:17). Moreover, the scriptures tell us that Jesus' sacrifice—while it is undeniably a "once-for-all" event—is nonetheless still ongoing. Or, perhaps better put, it exists out of time. For it is referred to in present tense in scripture, as is the need for the faithful to sacrifice on an ongoing basis.

Zech. 14:1-21 – "And every pot in Jerusalem and in Judah shall be holy to the Lord of hosts; and all who come to sacrifice shall take them and cook in them." This extended eschatological passage in Zechariah describes "the day of the Lord." It may be interpreted variously as either the end times, or the time after the arrival of the Messiah. Either way, the ongoing sacrifice by the faithful ones is clearly prophesied. Thus, the once-for-all sacrifice did not cease on the first Good Friday, but continues. Also note the interesting association between the sacrifice and a meal. The Eucharist, which is known to Catholics as a "sacrificial meal," is clearly foretold here.

Mal. 1:11 – "For from the rising of the sun, even to its setting, my name is great among the nations; and everywhere they bring sacrifice to my name, and a pure offering..." Again, the sacrifice by the faithful, through the eternal priesthood of Jesus, is ongoing. And note that this prophecy is fulfilled today. During every second of every day, the Holy Sacrifice of the Mass is being celebrated somewhere in the world.

1 Jn. 2:1-2 – "...If anyone does sin, we have an Advocate with the Father, Jesus Christ the righteous one. He is expiation for our sins, and not for our sins only but for those of the whole world." St. Paul is referring to the expiation of Christ's sacrifice in the present tense, not the past. Christ's role as Victim did not end two thousand years ago; his sacrifice is eternal, as we see in the following verse:

Rev. 5:6 – "Then I saw standing in the midst of the throne and the four living creatures and the elders a Lamb that seemed to have been slain." John's timeless vision of heaven includes Jesus' sacrifice—once again, not in past time but in the timeless present.

Ps. 110:4 – "Like Melchizedek you are a priest forever." This verse clearly establishes the Last Supper—and therefore the Mass—as a sacrifice. Since the Last Supper is the only point that Christ offers bread and wine, the Last Supper is the sole point of comparison between Melchizedek and Jesus. This compels us to conclude that Jesus was indeed acting as a "priest" at the Last Supper, and that his sacrifice is "forever." This very important verse is echoed in Heb. 5:6, 5:10, and 6:20.

1 Cor. 11:24 – "This cup is the new covenant in my blood. Do this, as often as you drink it, in remembrance of me." In recent centuries, Protestant thinkers have highlighted the word "remembrance" to bolster their view of the Sacrament of the Eucharist as symbol only. However, when an old friend visits—in person—we do a lot of recalling of old times together. This nostalgic sharing could certainly be termed a "remembrance." Loved ones can recall the past when they are together more easily than they can apart. So the word "remembrance" implies nothing about the Real Presence, pro or con. Fr. Mitch Pacwa, a popular author and scholar, says that the Greek word "anamnesis"—which we translate as "remembrance"—is a word that occurs very rarely in scripture and, when it does, is almost always associated with sacrifice. Outside of the context of the Last Supper, the word is found in the New Testament only in Heb. 10:3, where the "remembrance" is actually equated with the act of carrying out a sacrifice under the Mosaic law: "...in those sacrifices there is only the yearly remembrance of sins..." In the Old Testament, the word occurs in Lev. 23:24, where we find it translated as "reminder": "...you shall keep a sabbath rest, with a sacred assembly and with the trumpet blasts as a reminder, you shall then do no sort of work, and you shall offer an oblation to the Lord." Notice once again the context of sacrifice. And in Num. 10:10, we see the translation "reminder" again: "On your days of celebration, your festivals, and your new moon feasts, you shall blow the trumpet over your holocausts and your peace offerings; this will serve as a reminder of you before your God." Again, the clear reference is to "oblation," or sacrifice. So, if Jesus did not view the Last Supper—or the Mass—as a sacrifice, then he chose a very odd word—this "remembrance"—to instruct his followers to carry on the tradition. For when he says, "Do this in remembrance of me" he is making a crystal-clear reference to sacrifice, one that his followers could not possibly have overlooked.

Heb. 8:1-3 – "...We have such a high priest, who has taken his seat at the right hand of the throne of the Majesty in heaven, a minister of the sanctuary and of the true tabernacle that the Lord, not man, set up. Now every high priest is appointed to offer gifts and sacrifices; thus the necessity for this one also to have something to offer." Again, our high priest, Jesus, is offering sacrifice—present tense—in heaven. When a Catholic priest celebrates the Holy Sacrifice of the Mass, he and all present are joining in that heavenly sacrifice, with the heavenly hosts, and with Jesus as High Priest.

1 Cor. 5:7-8 – "For our paschal lamb, Christ has been sacrificed. Therefore, let us celebrate the feast..." Paul is referring to the Mass, the new Passover, where the people of God, united with the perfect sacrifice of Jesus through his Body and Blood in the Eucharist, pass over from sin and

death into the new life of salvation. The Church teaches that the Mass is both sacrifice and meal.

*From the earliest times, the community has been gathering to offer sacrifice—the Eucharistic liturgy. In 213 A.D., Tertullian wrote: "A woman, after the death of her husband…prays for his soul and asks that he may, while waiting, find rest; and that he may share in the first resurrection. And each year, on the anniversary of his death, she offers the sacrifice." (*The Faith of the Early Fathers,' *Vol. 1, William A. Jurgens, [Collegeville, Minnesota: Liturgical Press, 1970] p. 158.) This ancient text is an example of the memorial Mass, still offered today by Catholics for loved ones who have died. The reference to "sacrifice" is explicit throughout both the scriptures and the writings of the earliest believers. Yet most Protestant congregations today offer nothing remotely resembling a sacrifice.*

SUNDAY WORSHIP

God ordained a seven-day cycle for our lives—six days of work, followed by a day of rest. But nowhere in scripture is that cycle tied to any calendar system, let alone our own, which was not in existence until more than a thousand years later. God commands us to rest after a series of six days—not to rest on the specific day we now know as "Saturday." Indeed, during the time of the apostles, when the entire Church made the transition to worshiping on the Lord's Day rather than the Jewish Sabbath, not a single dissenting voice was raised among either the apostles or the early Church fathers. This fact alone validates the move.

Rev. 1:10 – St. John makes reference to the Lord's day, which proves that the focus shifted from "the seventh day" to "the eighth day" in apostolic times: "I was caught up in spirit on the Lord's day…"

Acts 20:7 – The Sunday Eucharist is referred to in the scriptures: "On the first day of the week when we gathered to break bread…" The very earliest believers went to the Jewish temple on the seventh day, then gathered as Christians on the next day, "the Lord's day," to break bread. As their sense of being people of the new covenant was refined, it became clear that they should dispense with the Mosaic law (see Gal. 4:10, below) and so they naturally transitioned to Sunday sabbathing. The fact that this took place in apostolic times, and that none of the apostles objected, means it was done through the authority of Jesus, who proclaimed himself Lord of the Sabbath (Mt. 12:8).

Gal. 4:10 – Paul exhorts the faithful to leave the Jewish observances behind: "You are observing days, months, seasons and years. I am afraid on your account that perhaps I have labored for you in vain."

1 Cor. 16:1-2 – "On the first day of the week each of you should set aside and save whatever he can afford..." St. Paul was collecting money for construction of a church in Jerusalem. Naturally, he requested that collections be taken up during the Eucharistic celebration which took place on "the first day of the week" rather than on the seventh. There is no question that the transition to Sunday sabbathing took place quite early and that the apostles sanctioned it.

Mt. 12:1-12 – The Pharisees object to the disciples breaking the Sabbath. Jesus corrects them: "I say to you, something greater than the temple is here...the Son of Man is Lord of the Sabbath." The Lord is linking the Jewish Sabbath observance with the Jewish temple, and making a clear distinction between himself and the temple, between the old covenant and the new.

Lev. 23:7; 23:16 – The Israelites actually celebrated the Sabbath on "Sunday," or "the eighth day," twice during the year. So even in Moses' time, it was accepted that under certain circumstances, the Sabbath could fall on a day other than the seventh.

Lk. 6:1-11 – The Pharisees protest that Jesus' followers desecrate the Sabbath; Jesus corrects them: "The Son of Man is lord of the Sabbath." To celebrate the Sabbath on the Lord's Day is simply an acknowledgment of the fact that, since our salvation by Jesus, we are newly created participants in the new covenant. As the original Sabbath honored God's creation of the universe as described in Genesis—the very creation that was stained by the sin of Adam and Eve—so Sunday sabbathing honors the new creation conceived through the death and resurrection of Christ. Denying the Sunday Sabbath celebration is to deny Christ his rightful place as Redeemer of the universe, because it denies the new creation which he instituted.

Lk. 13:10-17 – "Does not each one of you on the Sabbath untie his ox... This daughter of Abraham, whom Satan has bound for eighteen years now, ought she not to have been set free on the Sabbath day from this bondage?" Again, Jesus corrects a lack of understanding concerning the Sabbath. Clearly, Jesus' authority extends to the Sabbath.

Jn. 5:9-18 – "...The Jews began to persecute Jesus because he did this on a Sabbath. But Jesus answered them, 'My Father is at work until now, so I am at work.' For this reason the Jews tried all the more to kill him..." Jesus earned the enmity of Jewish authorities by reframing and redefining traditional Sabbath laws.

Ex. 16:1-30 – The Sabbath was instituted, not in reference to any specific day of the calendar, but in reference to a seemingly random day upon which the Israelites were grumbling against Moses and Aaron. "The Lord has given you the Sabbath. That is why on the sixth day he gives you food for two days. On the seventh day everyone is to stay home and no one is to go out." This is the inception of the Sabbath; no mention is made of the calendar, only of the cycle of six days of labor followed by a day of rest. The Jewish people themselves linked the Sabbath to the calendar, presumably for the sake of convenience. There is simply no biblical passage—and no divine injunction—that commands us to do so. Assigning the observation of the Sabbath to Saturday is a tradition instituted by men, not by God.

Ex. 35:1-3 – When Moses gives the people the Sabbath commandment, there is again no mention of any calendar system—only a cycle of six days' work, followed by one days' rest: "Moses assembled the whole Israelite community and said to them, 'This is what the Lord has commanded to be done. On six days work may be done, but the seventh day shall be sacred to you as the Sabbath of complete rest to the Lord.'"

Ex. 12:1-2 – The denominations that require Saturday sabbathing—despite the fact that there is no explicit command in scripture to do so—at the same time fail to follow this utterly explicit commandment which is categorically tied to the calendar: "The Lord said to Moses and Aaron in the land of Egypt, 'This month shall stand at the head of your calendar; you shall reckon it the first month of the year.'" This passage is referring to the month in which Passover falls, which of course is in the spring. Nonetheless, those denominations begin their annual count of months with January—not March, April or May—and in doing so ignore a commandment of the Lord that actually *is* about the calendar. Yet, as noted, by tying the cycle of six workdays followed by a day of rest to the calendar, they perceive a commandment where there is none.

Ezek. 20:10-12 – The Lord gave the Sabbath to the people in the desert after their exodus from Egypt, not immediately after creation week: "Therefore I led them out of the land of Egypt and brought them into the desert... I also gave them my sabbaths to be a sign between me and them, to show that it was I, the Lord, who made them holy." Again, there is no indication here that sabbathing is to be tied to a specific day of the week.

Mt. 20:19 – "...And he will be raised on the third day." If we are to interpret the Old Testament's command regarding sabbathing on "the seventh day" as being definitively tied to the calendar week, then must we not conclude that Jesus was here prophesying that his resurrection would take place on "the *third* day" of the week—or Tuesday? The resulting conclusion would be that Jesus was a false prophet, since the resurrection clearly did *not* take place on "the third day" of the week, but rather on "the first day." One interpretation is no more farfetched than the other.

Is. 1:13 – The letter of the old law gives way to the law of Jesus, which is written on our hearts: "New moon and sabbath, calling of assemblies, octaves with wickedness: these I cannot bear."

*Around the year 110 A.D., St. Ignatius, the third bishop of Antioch who was very likely instructed in the faith by the apostles Peter and John, confirms the fact that the early Christians no longer gathered with the Jewish community on Saturday, but instead celebrated the resurrection by worshiping on Sunday: "If, then, those who walked in ancient customs came to a new hope, no longer sabbathing but living by the Lord's Day, on which we came to life through Him and through His death..." (*The Faith of the Early Fathers,' Vol. 1, William A. Jurgens, [Collegeville, Minnesota: Liturgical Press, 1970] p. 19).*

If Sunday worship is the sign of apostasy, as some denominations claim, then how is it that the entire community fell into sin almost instantly, contrary to Jesus' promise that the gates of the netherworld would not prevail against his Church (Mt. 16:18), and how is it that the Holy Spirit worked through apostates to reveal to them precisely which books ought to be included in the canon of scripture and which should not? And where are the writings of those who remained faithful to the practices taught by the apostles? No, it is too much to believe that the entire Church simultaneously and spontaneously apostatized en masse, and that those who were instructed in the faith by the lips of the apostles themselves were the authors of this mass apostasy. (See the "Great Apostasy" section below.)

SCHISM/APOSTASY

Even non-Christian faith traditions recognize the value to a soul of submitting to a spiritual authority greater than oneself. Yet the Protestant doctrine of "sola scriptura," which gives ultimate spiritual authority to each individual's interpretation of scripture, makes such submission unnecessary. It also guarantees that there will be an ongoing proliferation of denominations and sects, as each new and different subset of interpretations seeks to assert itself. In short, "sola scriptura" makes schism inevitable. Yet the Bible clearly reveals that schism is against God's will:

Acts 17:30 – "God has overlooked the times of ignorance, but now he demands that all people everywhere repent because he has established a day on which he will 'judge the world with justice' through a man he has appointed, and he has provided confirmation for all by raising him from the dead." The times of ignorance are over; God has shown us the way through his Son, Jesus Christ. We have no excuse for not following him and the Church he founded.

Rom. 13:1-2 – "Let every person be subordinate to the higher authorities, for there is no authority except from God, and those that exist have been established by God. Therefore, whoever resists authority opposes what God has appointed, and those who oppose it will bring judgment upon themselves." St. Paul could scarcely be clearer. When we submit to the spiritual authorities ordained by God, we are in truth submitting to God himself.

Jer. 14:15-16 – "Therefore, thus says the Lord: 'Concerning the prophets who prophesy in my name, though I did not send them...by the sword and famine shall these prophets meet their end. The people to whom they prophesy shall be cast out into the streets of Jerusalem by famine and the sword. No one shall bury them, their wives, their sons, or their daughters, for I will pour out upon them their own wickedness.'" It is a bad thing to follow a false prophet, and worse yet to be one.

Mk. 13:21-22 – "False messiahs and false prophets will arise and will perform signs and wonders in order to mislead... Be watchful! I have told it all to you beforehand." We must always ask by what authority spiritual leaders lead.

2 Pet. 2:1-2 – "...There will be false teachers among you, who will introduce destructive heresies and even deny the Master who ransomed them, bringing swift destruction on themselves. Many will follow their licentious ways..." All of the great heretics of history have come from the ranks of the clergy of the Catholic Church. This fact fulfills Jesus' prophecy, which says the false teachers who introduce destructive heresies will be "among" the faithful.

Mt. 7:15-20 – "Beware of false prophets, who come to you in sheep's clothing, but underneath are ravenous wolves." The false prophets will not necessarily be readily identifiable. Some may appear learned or pious or educated in the scriptures.

Ezek. 22:28 – There are false prophets who invoke the name of God: "...pretending to visions that are false and performing lying divinations, saying, 'Thus says the Lord God,' although the Lord has not spoken."

Rev. 2:15-16 – "...You also have some people who hold to the teaching of [the] Nicolaitans. Therefore, repent. Otherwise, I will come to you quickly and wage war against them with the sword of my mouth." The Lord himself will assail those who adhere to error.

Tit. 3:10-11 – Heretics are to be avoided: "After a first and second warning, break off contact with a heretic, realizing that such a person is perverted and sinful and stands self-condemned."

1 Jn. 2:19 – "They went out from us, but they were not really of our number; if they had been, they would have remained with us. Their desertion shows that none of them was of our number." St. John is telling us quite clearly that it is submission to apostolic authority that is the chief hallmark of faithfulness—*not*, it is worth pointing out, one's own deftness at interpreting scriptures.

1 Jn. 4:6 – "...Anyone who knows God listens to us, while anyone who does not belong to God refuses to hear us. This is how we know the spirit of truth and the spirit of deceit." The ultimate sign of truth is apostolic authority. Those whose beliefs depart from the teachings of the apostles—which we discern through both the scriptures and through Sacred Tradition, as defined by the Magisterium of the Church and the testimony of the early Church fathers who themselves learned the faith from the lips of the apostles—do not belong to God.

Deut. 17:8-12 – "Any man who has the insolence to refuse to listen to the priest...shall die." Submission to spiritual authority ordained by God has always been a requirement—indeed, a hallmark—of the chosen. Proclaiming ourselves—or our own interpretations of scripture—as the supreme authority of faith places us in mortal danger.

2 Cor. 6:14-15 – "Do not be yoked with those who are different, with unbelievers. For what partnership do righteousness and lawlessness have? Or what fellowship does light have with darkness?"

Num. 12:1-15 – Miriam rebels: "Is it through Moses alone that the Lord speaks? Does he not speak through us also?" Miriam is rendered leprous for her sin. Her complaint sounds remarkably like the sentiments of many Christians today who dispute the authority of the Church hierarchy. Of course we know that the Bible refers to the "kingdom" of God, not the "committee" of God, nor the "co-op" of God.

Num. 16:1-35 – The ancient scriptural account of the revolt of Korah contains this rallying cry that could have been written by the 16th century Reformers as they railed against the authority of the Catholic Church: "They stood before Moses and held an assembly against Moses and Aaron, to whom they said, 'Enough from you! The whole community, all of them, are holy; the Lord is in their midst. Why then should you set yourselves over the Lord's congregation?' ...So they withdrew from the space around the Dwelling... And fire from the Lord came forth which consumed the two hundred and fifty men..." The Lord's wrath is unleashed against those who would question the authority of the leaders he ordains.

Rom. 10:3 – "...In their unawareness of the righteousness that comes from God and their attempt to establish their own [righteousness], they did not submit to the righteousness of God." Submission is one of the keys to the spiritual life—submission to God and to his ordained authority on earth, the Church. People who try to find their own way, trusting to their own understanding of God's revelation rather than to the collective wisdom of centuries, run the gravest of risks.

The 2000 edition of the World Christian Encyclopedia, published by Oxford University Press, estimates that there are 33,820 Christian denominations. And these separate groups do not all agree on a single tenet of faith, with the possible exception of heaven (although they strenuously disagree on who will gain entry). This cannot be the unity Jesus petitioned from the Father before he died (see John 17).

THE "GREAT APOSTASY"

Mormons, Seventh Day Adventists and various other non-Catholic groups claim that in the days immediately after Jesus' Ascension, the Catholic Church apostatized en masse. One problem with this theory is that, if it is true, then Jesus' promise not to let the netherworld prevail against his Church (Mt. 16:15-19) was false—which we know cannot be the case. Another problem is that the early Church fathers are nearly uniform in their understandings of the faith. If their teachings are non-apostolic, then where are the writings of those who remained firm in the faith of the apostles and disputed these false teachings? There are no such writings. No, for more than a thousand years after Jesus, the understanding of Christian believers on so many of the questions that are now in dispute—infant Baptism, Jesus' Real Presence in the Holy Eucharist, Sunday worship, Mary's role in salvation history, etc.—were uniformly adhered to in the Church our Lord founded. There were simply no voices in the early Church that questioned them. It is impossible to conceive of these early believers undermining the faith which they received from the apostles' own lips by developing their own doctrines. After all, in so many cases, their commitment to their faith was absolute and unwavering. Rather than compromise its purity by offering even a thimbleful of incense to the Roman gods, they chose instead to suffer torture and death as martyrs to their faith. It is difficult to imagine a more resolute commitment to the truth than what these holy men and women demonstrated, even at the cost of their lives.

Acts 20:29-30 – "I know that after my departure savage wolves will come among you, and they will not spare the flock. And from your own group, men will come forward perverting the truth to draw the disciples away after them." Many point to this passage as a prophecy of "the great apostasy" of the early Catholic Church. However, in no way does this passage predict the apostasy of the entire early Christian community. For the "wolves" are said to come "among" the believers. So many must have remained faithful to Jesus' authentic teachings for there to have been "believers" for the wolves to come among. Indeed, this prophecy arguably was fulfilled when two Catholic clergymen left the Church to become the two greatest heresiarchs of history— Arius and Luther. Both men originated from "among" the faithful, since both were Catholic clergy before their apostasy. This applies to many of the other schismatics of history as well—Marcion, Calvin, Lefebvre, etc.

2 Pet. 2:1-2 – "...There will be false teachers among you, who will introduce destructive heresies and even deny the Master who ransomed them, bringing swift destruction on themselves. Many will follow their licentious ways and because of them the way of truth will be reviled." Again, this cannot be a prophecy of the entire Church apostatizing, since the "false teachers" will be found "among you"—which is to say, among the true community of believers. Thus, the teachers are false, not the community. Again, Marcion, Arius and Luther would each seem to qualify quite nicely as fulfilling this prophecy, for each was definitely "among" the faithful, having been a member of the Catholic clergy before having become a schismatic.

Mt. 28:18-20 – "All power in heaven and on earth has been given to me. Go, therefore, and make disciples of all nations, baptizing them... teaching them to observe all I have commanded you. And behold, I am with you always, until the end of the world." Jesus promised to be with his Church until the end of time, so we can be assured it will never fail.

CALL NO MAN "FATHER"

This command of Jesus, found in Mt. 23:9-10, is not about vocabulary. If it were, the New Testament writers wouldn't have repeatedly used the word "Father" to refer to human beings. Instead, Jesus is warning us against putting our complete faith and trust in a human being rather than God. We must never submit our innermost being to anyone other than God himself. No prophet, no guru, no teacher should garner our total trust, only God. If simply using the word, "Father," to refer to a human being were wrong, we would not find the word used that way throughout the scripture. But of course we do—again and again.

Lk. 16:24 – Jesus himself refers to "Father Abraham" in the parable of Lazarus the beggar. Would he have failed to follow his own command?

1 Cor. 4:14-15 – "…I became your father in Christ through the gospel…" St. Paul refers to himself as a spiritual father. In doing so, he defines the way in which Catholics use the term "father" in referring to a priest—as a "father in Christ through the gospel."

Acts 7:1-2 – St. Stephen, the first martyr, says to the high priest and the elders and scribes: "My brothers and fathers, listen. The God of glory appeared to our father Abraham…"

Rom. 4:17-18 – St. Paul refers to Abraham as "… the father of us all…" and "the father of many nations."

1 Thess. 2:11 – "…We treated each one of you as a father treats his children…" Again, St. Paul describes himself as a spiritual father to the faithful.

1 Jn. 2:13-14 – "I write to you, fathers…" St. John also appears to disobey Jesus' directive—an impossibility, of course. So we see that the vocabulary-based interpretation of Jesus' admonition cannot be correct.

Mt. 23:8 – Actually, "father" is not the only word which the passage in question appears to forbid us from using: "As for you, do not be called 'Rabbi.' You have but one teacher, and you are all brothers." "Rabbi" means "teacher." Yet the same people who object to priests being called "father" don't blink an eye when they refer to their Sunday school "teachers."

UNITY

There is no indication in scripture that Jesus planned for his followers to be divided into separate denominations, divided by different traditions and beliefs, divided on virtually every single Christian doctrine including the divinity of Jesus himself. Instead, we see the Lord praying that his followers be united in their faith. The Protestant notion that the Church referred to in the New Testament is "invisible"—in fact, imaginary—is found nowhere in the scriptures. It is another innovation, a "tradition of men."

Jn. 17:11-23 – "I pray not only for them, but also for those who will believe in me through their word, so that they may all be one, as you, Father, are in me and I in you, that they also may be in us, that the world may believe that you sent me." Jesus is upholding the union of all believers in the communion of saints, saying we are one in the same way he and the Father are one. What an awesome, profound prayer this is, and glorious will be the day when it reaches its ultimate fulfillment.

Phil. 1:27-28 – "…Standing firm in one spirit, with one mind struggling together for the faith of the gospel, not intimidated in any way by your opponents. This is proof to them of destruction, but of your salvation." The divisions that plague the "sola scriptura" congregations—on matters as basic as the nature of Jesus himself—are convincing evidence that the Holy Spirit is not guiding them.

Phil. 2:2 – "…Complete my joy by being of the same mind, with the same love, united in heart, thinking one thing." The idea of multiple denominations would not have been appealing to St. Paul.

1 Jn. 2:19 – "They went out from us, but they were not really of our number; if they had been, they would have remained with us. Their desertion shows that none of them was of our number." Submission to apostolic authority is a hallmark of faith.

THE ROSARY/VAIN REPETITIONS

When we Catholics pray the Rosary, Protestants accuse us of disobeying Mt. 6:7, which states, "In praying, do not babble like the pagans, who think that they will be heard because of their many words." But the Rosary is scripture-based, and in praying it we are not emulating pagans, but the heavenly hosts:

Rev. 4:8 – "Day and night they do not stop exclaiming: 'Holy, holy, holy is the Lord God almighty, who was, and who is, and who is to come.'" St. John's vision of heaven revealed that the angels and saints pray repetitively. So obviously Jesus was objecting not to repetition, but to the insincerity and emptiness of the pagans' words.

And of course the prayers of the Rosary, the "Hail Mary" and the "Our Father," are both scripture-based. If we are wrong to pray the "Hail Mary," then so was the Angel Gabriel who first "prayed" it (see Luke Chapter 1).

GRAVEN IMAGES

The word, "graven," means cut, chiseled, or engraved. God's commandment against graven images refers to the worship of idols shaped by human hands, in the style of the pagans. It clearly did not mean that all images are inherently evil—neither statues in churches, nor photos in wallets. In fact, on many occasions God himself specifically directs the Israelites to fashion images of various types. So clearly it is the worship of such images that is an abomination, not the images themselves.

Ex. 25:18 – God directed the Israelites to decorate the ark of the covenant with images of angels: "Make two cherubim of beaten gold for the two ends of the propitiatory, fastening them so that one cherub springs direct from each end. The cherubim shall have their wings spread out above..."

Ex. 37:7-9 – "Two cherubim of beaten gold were made for the two ends of the propitiatory... They were turned toward each other, but with their faces looking toward the propitiatory."

2 Chron. 3:10-13 – "Graven images" of angels were constructed for the temple as well: "For the room of the holy of holies he made two cherubim of carved workmanship which were then overlaid with gold. The wings of the cherubim spanned twenty cubits..." This could never have been permitted if images were forbidden by God.

2 Chron. 4:4 – Figures of twelve metal oxen stood in temple: "It rested on twelve oxen, three facing north, three west, three south, and three east, with their haunches all toward the center..."

1 Kings 7:29 – There was a large assortment of images visible in the temple: "On the panels between the frames there were lions, oxen, and cherubim; and on the frames likewise, above and below the lions and oxen, there were wreaths in relief."

1 Kings 6:23 – Under his own volition, Solomon had cherubim made for the temple; God did not command it, but neither was their presence offensive to him: "In the sanctuary were two cherubim, each ten cubits high, made of olive wood." Also, it is quite clear that any images of wood must have been "graven."

Ezek. 41:17-18 – "...On every wall on every side in both the inner and outer rooms were carved the figures of cherubim and palm trees..."

Heb. 9:5 – In the New Testament as well, images of angels were said to have adorned the temple: "Above it were the cherubim of glory overshadowing the place of expiation." They could scarcely have been offensive to God.

Ex. 26:31 – Embroidered images were also fashioned for the sanctuary of the ark: "You shall have a veil woven of violet, purple and scarlet yarn, and of fine linen twined, with cherubim embroidered on it."

Num. 21:8 – "...the Lord said to Moses, 'Make a saraph and mount it on a pole, and if anyone who has been bitten looks at it, he will recover.' Moses accordingly made a bronze serpent and mounted it on a pole..." This is, *prima facie,* a violation of the supposed injunction against fashioning images of creatures, yet God himself commands it. So clearly the literalist interpretation—that any fashioning of images of creatures is offensive to God—must be faulty. And note the New Testament reference to this event:

Jn. 3:14-15 – "And just as Moses lifted up the serpent in the desert, so must the Son of Man be lifted up, so that everyone who believes in him may have eternal life." The Israelites were saved after Moses followed God's directive and fashioned a figure of a snake and held it up before the people. It is thus quite obvious that the commandment did not forbid all images of physical beings.

Is. 45:20 – "They are without knowledge who bear wooden idols and pray to gods that cannot save." It is the worship of false gods that is forbidden, not the simple fashioning of images. Nowhere do the scriptures actually forbid us from fashioning images, graven or otherwise. They merely forbid us from worshiping images, which of course no Christian could ever conceive of doing.

VENERATING RELICS

The understanding that certain objects became holy through their proximity with God or with a holy person predates Jesus by centuries. Witness the power associated with the ark of the covenant, and the reverence accorded it. We also see holy objects venerated in the New Testament as well.

2 Kings 13:21 – "Elisha died and was buried. At the time, bands of Moabites used to raid the land each year. Once some people were burying a man, when suddenly they spied such a raiding band. So they cast the dead man into the grave of Elisha, and everyone went off. But when the man came in contact with the bones of Elisha, he came back to life and rose to his feet." This is an example of the relics of a holy man actually bringing the dead to life.

Acts 19:11-12 – Scripture tells us that, through the grace of God, material items can convey his power. For example, objects which St. Paul touched actually healed the sick: "So extraordinary were the mighty deeds God accomplished at the hands of Paul that when face cloths or aprons that touched his skin were applied to the sick, their diseases left them..."

Mt. 9:20 – "A woman suffering hemorrhages for twelve years came up behind him and touched the tassel on his cloak. She said to herself, 'If only I can touch his cloak, I will be cured'..." The cloak did not have power in its own right, but through the One who was wearing it. Yet "faith alone" did not succeed in healing the suffering woman—for faith was what inspired her to touch the cloak. She had to step forward in faith and *touch*. It was her faith in Jesus, combined with her action, that yielded the cure.

Mt. 14:35-36 – "People brought to him all those who were sick and begged him that they might touch only the tassel on his cloak, and as many as touched it were healed."

The earliest detailed account we have of martyrdom outside that of Stephen in Acts 7 is that of the venerable saint, Polycarp, in 155 A.D. Even at this early date, we see the faithful preserving and revering the relics of this beloved man: "When the centurion saw the contentiousness caused by the Jews, he confiscated the body and, according to their custom, burned it. Then, at last, we took up his bones, more precious than costly gems and finer than gold, and put them in a suitable place. The Lord will permit us, when we are able, to assemble there in joy and gladness; and to celebrate the birthday of his martyrdom, both in memory of those who have already engaged in the contest, and for the practice and training of those who have yet to fight." (The Faith of the Early Fathers, *Vol. 1, William A. Jurgens,[Collegeville, Minnesota: Liturgical Press, 1970] p. 31.) Note also the very ancient practice of celebrating feast days.*

CRUCIFIXES

The crucifix is a symbol of the Paschal mystery, which tells us that, to share in the victory of the resurrection, we must unite our suffering with that of the Lord in his Passion. We are reminded—vividly—that there is no birth to new life without a death to the old. This is a difficult message for us to accept, of course, which is why we need it constantly before us.

Num. 15:37-41 – This command from God shows that the sight of a physical object can turn one's heart toward holy things: "The Lord said to Moses, 'Speak to the Israelites and tell them that they and their descendants must put tassels on the corners of their garments, fastening each corner tassel with a violet cord. When you use these tassels, let the sight of them remind you to keep all the commandments of the Lord, without going wantonly astray after the desires of your hearts and eyes. Thus you will remember to keep all my commandments and be holy to your God.'"

2 Tim. 2:11-12 – "If we have died with him we shall also live with him; if we persevere we shall also reign with him." The crucifix is a reminder of this supremely important fact. Our salvation depends utterly on the cross of Jesus, just as the blood on the lintel—a precursor of the cross, according to the early Church fathers—was the salvation of the firstborn of Israel at the first Passover.

Mt. 10:38 – "...Whoever does not take up his cross and follow after me is not worthy of me." Jesus himself repeatedly reminds us of his cross. Will we turn away from it, or will we embrace it? This is the question posed by every crucifix we see.

Gal. 6:14 – "But may I never boast except in the cross of our Lord Jesus Christ, through which the world has been crucified to me, and I to the world." Christians who display the crucifix are doing nothing more than following the example of St. Paul and boasting—visually—in the cross of our Lord.

PERSECUTION

Unfortunately, many who decide to convert from Protestant denominations to the Catholic faith suffer abuse from well intentioned, but misguided, family and friends. Jesus tells us that following him entails a price. Anyone who suffers persecution for his sake is in a very real sense a martyr for the Lord.

Mt. 5:11-12 – "Blessed are you when they insult you and persecute you and utter every kind of evil against you [falsely] because of me. Rejoice and be glad, for your reward will be great in heaven."

Mt. 10:21-23 – "Brother will hand over brother to death, and the father his child; children will rise up against parents and have them put to death. You will be hated by all because of my name, but whoever endures to the end will be saved." Some of the worst examples of persecution occur within families, as Jesus said would occur.

Mt. 10:25-33 – "If they have called the master of the house Beelzebul, how much more those of his household!... Everyone who acknowledges me before others I will acknowledge before my heavenly father. But whoever denies me before others, I will deny before my heavenly father." It is no accident that many characterize the Catholic Church as the Antichrist and the "whore of Babylon." They said the same kinds of things about her founder and head, Jesus. When people say these things, they are merely fulfilling Jesus' own prophetic words. And when we have the opportunity to stand firm for our faith in the face of strong opposition—or even persecution—we will be acknowledged by our Savior in heaven. So, difficult though it may be, we should be grateful when we are attacked for our faith.

Mt. 10:37-39 – "Whoever loves father or mother more than me is not worthy of me, and whoever loves son or daughter more than me is not worthy of me; and whoever does not take up his cross and follow after me is not worthy of me. Whoever finds his life will lose it, and whoever loses his life for my sake will find it." Those who are persecuted for their faith are the most fortunate of Christians, for they are able to prove beyond question their love for Jesus.

Jn. 15:18-16:2 – "If the world hates you, realize that it hated me first… the hour is coming when everyone who kills you will think he is offering worship to God. They will do this because they have not known either the Father or me. I have told you this so that when their hour comes you may remember that I told you." Jesus warns us to expect opposition and hatred—and, on occasion, death.

GUARDIAN ANGELS

Many people feel guardian angels are like fairies and unicorns—a harmless fiction told to children. Yet the teaching about guardian angels has a solid biblical foundation.

Mt. 18:10 – "…do not despise one of these little ones, for I say to you that their angels in heaven always look upon the face of my heavenly Father." Here Jesus himself upholds the existence of guardian angels who watch over children.

Ps. 91:11-12 – "For God commands the angels to guard you in all your ways. With their hands they shall support you…"

Heb. 1:13-14 – "…to which of the angels has he ever said: 'Sit at my right hand until I make your enemies your footstool?' Are they not all ministering spirits sent to serve, for the sake of those who are to inherit salvation?"

Ps. 34:8 – "The angel of the Lord, who encamps with them, delivers all who fear God."

Dan. 6:23 – "'My God has sent his angel and closed the lions' mouths so that they have not hurt me.'"

Acts 5:19 – "…During the night, the angel of the Lord opened the doors of the prison, led them out, and said, 'Go and take your place in the temple area, and tell the people everything about this life.'"

EXCOMMUNICATION

Since apostolic times, divisive influences within the community were summarily expelled. This practice is both advocated and practiced in the Bible.

1 Tim. 1:20 – "…Hymenaeus and Alexander, whom I have handed over to Satan to be taught how not to blaspheme." St. Paul himself expelled evildoers from the community.

Mt. 16:19 – "Whatever you bind on earth will be bound in heaven; and whatever you loose on earth shall be loosed in heaven." Jesus promises that whatever approbations or condemnations are issued by the Church will be honored in heaven.

Mt. 18:17-18 – "If he refuses to listen even to the church, then treat him as you would a Gentile or a tax collector. Amen, I say to you, whatever you bind on earth shall be bound in heaven..." Jesus instructs his followers to eject stubborn offenders from their midst.

1 Cor. 16:22 – "If anyone does not love the Lord, let him be accursed."

DIETARY LAWS & ALCOHOL AS SIN

The Protestant communities that forbid alcohol consumption claim to uphold the principle of "sola scriptura." Yet nowhere do we see the scriptures forbidding consumption of alcohol. Indeed, as we know, Jesus' first miracle was the changing of water into wine. There is an important distinction between forbidding drunkenness, which the Bible does, and forbidding alcohol, which the Bible does not.

1 Tim. 5:23 – "Stop drinking water, but have a little wine for the sake of your stomach..." Would St. Paul have made this recommendation if drinking alcohol were an offense to God?

1 Tim. 4:3 – "They forbid marriage and require abstinence from foods that God created to be received with thanksgiving..." We can conclude from this statement of St. Paul's that the very fact that certain groups outlaw the eating of certain foods is an indication that they are not of the true faith.

Col. 2:20-23 – "...Why do you submit to regulations as if you were still living in the world? 'Do not handle! Do not taste! Do not touch!' These are all things destined to perish with use; they accord with human precepts and teachings. While they have a semblance of wisdom in rigor of devotion and self-abasement and severity to the body, they are of no value against gratification of the flesh." One of the signs of a faith tradition that is unbiblical is the prohibition of certain kinds of food and drink.

CELIBACY

Some Protestants claim that 1 Tim. 4:1-3, which condemns those who forbid marriage, refers to the tradition of priestly celibacy within the Latin Rite of the Catholic Church. But this is false, since the Church does not coerce anyone to be a priest or a sister. Anyone is free to choose the married life as a vocation. Nonetheless, St. Paul is definite about the efficacy of the celibate state. For those able to conquer their natural desires, celibacy is the preferred lifestyle of one who seeks to commit his or her life to God. When Luther decried celibacy on the grounds that it was too difficult, he contradicted scripture's clearly stated position.

1 Cor. 7:32-35 – "An unmarried man is anxious about the things of the Lord, how he may please the Lord. But a married man is anxious about the things of the world, how he may please his wife, and he is divided. An unmarried woman or a virgin is anxious about the things of the Lord, so that she may be holy in both body and spirit. A married woman, on the other hand, is anxious about the things of the world, how she may please her husband." St. Paul is definite: For the spiritual person who is able to manage it, celibacy is the preferred way of life. It allows one's commitment to the Lord to remain undivided.

Mt. 19:12 – "Some are incapable of marriage because they were born so; some, because they were made so by others; some, because they have renounced marriage for the sake of the kingdom of heaven. Whoever can accept this ought to accept it." Jesus himself holds up celibacy—the renunciation of marriage for the kingdom of heaven—as admirable.

1 Cor. 7:37-38 – "The one who stands firm in his resolve, however, who is not under compulsion but has power over his own will, and has made up his mind to keep his virgin, will be doing well. So then, the one who marries his virgin does well; the one who does not marry her will do better."

Jer. 16:1-2 – Jeremiah was commanded by God to live a celibate life: "This message came to me from the Lord: Do not marry any woman; you shall not have sons or daughters in this place..."

Ex. 19:15 – God commanded his people to abstain from intercourse during great and holy events, in this case the coming of the Lord down from Mt. Sinai: "...[Moses] warned them, 'Be ready for the third day. Have no intercourse with any woman.'"

1 Sam. 21:4-5 – The priest Abimelech stipulates that the holy bread which he gives to David may be eaten only by men who have abstained from intercourse.

ASH WEDNESDAY/LENTON DEVOTIONS

Fasting and penance were used by the ancients to express contrition, and to assist them in controlling their natural urges. This message of humble self-abnegation runs counter to our culture's emphasis on satisfying any and every desire we might feel. The Church's penitential traditions are intended to help us become more conscious of—and more contrite about—our sins, as well as to help us conquer our impulses and desires as the holy ones did in ancient times.

Gen. 18:27 – "Abraham spoke up again... 'I am but dust and ashes.'" The Ash Wednesday devotions are intended simply to remind us of this fact.

2 Sam. 13:19 – "Tamar put ashes on her head and tore the long tunic in which she was clothed..."

Esther 4:1-3 – "When Mordecai learned all that was happening, he tore his garments, put on sackcloth and ashes..."

Dan. 9:3 – "I turned to the Lord God, pleading in earnest prayer, with fasting, sackcloth, and ashes. I prayed to the Lord, my God, and confessed..."

Job. 42:6 – "Therefore I disown what I have said, and repent in dust and ashes."

Jon. 3:6-10 – "When the news reached the king of Nineveh, he rose from his throne, laid aside his robe, covered himself with sackcloth and sat in the ashes. Then he had this proclaimed throughout Nineveh... 'Neither man nor beast, neither cattle nor sheep, shall taste anything; they shall not eat, nor shall they drink water.' ...When God saw by their actions how they turned from their evil way, he repented of the evil that he had threatened to do to them; he did not carry it out."

Mt. 3:1-6 – "In those days, John the Baptist appeared, preaching in the desert of Judea [and] saying, 'Repent, for the kingdom of heaven is at hand!'... John wore clothing made of camel's hair and had a leather belt around his waist. His food was locusts and wild honey..." Throughout the scriptures, we see the holy ones undergoing great self-denial. Lent is an opportunity for all of us to examine our lives and take steps to cleanse our hearts and our lives of distractions and impediments.

Mt. 4:2 – "He fasted for forty days and forty nights, and afterwards he was hungry." Jesus himself denied his bodily appetites.

Lk. 10:13 – "Woe to you, Chorazin! Woe to you, Bethsaida! For if the mighty deeds done in your midst had been done in Tyre and Sidon, they would long ago have repented, sitting in sackcloth and ashes." Doing penance has always been a part of repentance.

Mt. 11:21 – "Woe to you, Chorazin! Woe to you, Bethsaida! For if the mighty deeds done in your midst had been done in Tyre and Sidon, they would long ago have repented in sackcloth and ashes." Scriptures repeat the above passage in which Jesus acknowledges—and thus endorses—the practice of doing penance for one's offenses.

Ezek. 9:1-11 – The foreheads of the just ones who recoil at the evil of the world are marked with the sign of the Lord. The evildoers are killed, but the ones whose foreheads are marked are spared.

THE DIVINITY OF JESUS

Some faith traditions, including Jehovah's Witnesses, have revisited the ancient Arian heresy, denying Jesus' divinity and viewing him as a created being, an exalted figure whose nature is somewhere between man's and God's. They point to verses such as, "…the Father is greater than I" (Jn. 14:28); "…I am going to my Father and your Father, to my God and your God" (Jn. 20:17) and, "…Christ is the head of every man, and a husband the head of his wife, and God the head of Christ" (1 Cor. 11:3). These—and other—passages seem convincing, at least until one examines the verses that flatly contradict this interpretation, several of which are represented below. How can we reconcile these two pictures—Jesus as clearly subject to the Father, and Jesus as One with the Father? Easily, for even though any human father is in a certain sense "greater" than his son, they are also co-equals in terms of their nature and substance. In addition, Jesus is both man and God. Certainly, in his human nature, he is created and is thus subject to the Father. But to focus solely on his human nature to the exclusion of his place in the Godhead is a complete mischaracterization of Jesus' true nature—and an express denial of another entire set of Bible verses. In addition, many of the passages cited by the opponents of the Trinity—including Mt. 3:17, where we find the Father saying, "This is my beloved Son, with whom I am well pleased"—illustrate only that Jesus is God's Son, and not that he is inferior at all. In fact in Jn. 5:18, we find that being God's Son actually means being equal to God: "For this reason the Jews tried all the more to kill him, because he not only broke the Sabbath but he also called God his own father, making himself equal to God." The fact is, Jesus was quite explicit about who he is and why he came. If he was wrong—or if he was lying—then the temple leaders were totally justified in executing him.

Acts 20:28 – "…You tend the church of God that he acquired with his own blood." In this passage, "God" is the only possible antecedent of the pronoun "he." Thus, St. Paul is clearly stating that Jesus is God, for Jesus is the one whose blood was shed.

Jn. 1:1-3 – "In the beginning was the Word, and the Word was with God, and the Word was God. He was in the beginning with God. All things came to be through him, and without him nothing came to be." Jesus, the Son, is the Word. In the beginning he was both "God" and "with God." This is a simple, poetic statement of the relationship of the Trinity: "God with God." Also, the fact that all was created through the Son— and that "without him nothing came to be"—is a clear statement that Jesus is himself not a creature. Since all of creation—including each and every creature—came to be through him, we must conclude that Jesus himself is not a creature, or it would mean he had to have created himself, an obvious impossibility.

Rev. 3:14 – "To the angel of the church in Laodicea write this: 'The Amen, the faithful and true witness, the source of God's creation...'" Again, we see that Jesus was the source of all creation. Therefore—by definition, even—he cannot himself be a creature.

Jn. 8:58 – Jesus makes his nature clear: "'Amen, amen, I say to you, before Abraham came to be, I AM.' So they picked up stones to throw at him; but Jesus hid and went out of the temple area." The great "I AM" was the sacred name taken by Yahweh. Jesus is stating his nature in terms so clear and strong that, if wrong, they would totally justify his execution. Which is why those present immediately tried to stone him. They were very clear on the divine nature he was claiming.

Acts 7:59 – In scripture, we see the faithful actually praying to Jesus: "As they were stoning Stephen, he called out, 'Lord Jesus, receive my spirit.'" Again, this is a clear indication of Jesus' divinity.

1 Cor. 1:2-3 – "...To you who have been sanctified in Christ Jesus, called to be holy, with all those everywhere who call upon the name of our Lord Jesus Christ, their Lord and ours. Grace to you and peace from God our Father and the Lord Jesus Christ." St. Paul is definite about whose name the faithful are to call upon.

2 Pet. 1:1 – "...To those who have received a faith of equal value to ours through the righteousness of our God and savior, Jesus Christ..." Peter could scarcely be more explicit about the divinity of Jesus.

Jn. 10:30-33 – "'The Father and I are one.' The Jews again picked up rocks to stone him. Jesus answered them, 'I have shown you many good works from my Father. For which of these are you trying to stone me?' The Jews answered him, 'We are not stoning you for a good work but for blasphemy. You, a man, are making yourself God.'" The Jews knew the significance of Jesus' statements about his nature. They were absolutely right about his claims. His only possible defense, of course, was that his claims were true.

Jn. 5:18 – "For this reason the Jews tried all the more to kill him, because he not only broke the Sabbath but he also called God his own father, making himself equal to God." If Jesus' divinity was nothing more than a misunderstanding perpetuated by his followers years after his death, then why did he not correct the same idea held by the temple authorities in the passage above, and thus avoid a wretched and painful death?

Lk. 10:18 – "Jesus said, 'I have observed Satan fall like lightning from the sky. Behold, I have given you the power 'to tread upon serpents' and scorpions and upon the full force of the enemy and nothing will harm you.'" Jesus tells us he is the one who imparts these supernatural powers to his followers. He does not ask the Father to impart them; he does not need to. He is God. Not one of the prophets, kings and judges of the Bible—not Abraham, not Moses, not David — ever made a similar claim.

Phil. 2:6-7 – "…Christ Jesus, who though he was in the form of God, did not regard equality with God something to be grasped. Rather he emptied himself, taking the form of a slave, coming in human likeness; and found human in appearance, he humbled himself…" This is an explicit statement that Jesus was consubstantial—or "One in Being," as the ancient Nicene Creed puts it—with the Father.

Mt. 11:27 – "All things have been handed over to me by my Father. No one knows the Son except the Father, and no one knows the Father except the Son and any one to whom the Son wishes to reveal him."

Jn. 14:6-10 – "Do you not believe that I am in the Father and the Father is in me? The words that I speak to you I do not speak on my own. The Father who dwells in me is doing his works. Believe me that I am in the Father and the Father is in me, or else, believe because of the works themselves."

Jn. 17:3 – Jesus' prayer reveals his true nature: "Now this is eternal life, that they should know you, the only true God, and the one whom you sent, Jesus Christ. I glorified you on earth by accomplishing the work that you gave me to do. Now glorify me, Father, with you, with the glory that I had with you before the world began."

Rev. 22:13 – "I am the Alpha and the Omega, the first and the last, the beginning and the end." Christ refers to himself with the very phrase spoken by God in scripture to describe himself (Is. 41:4 and 44:6; Rev. 1:8 and 21:6). Jesus' meaning could scarcely be clearer.

As evidence of Jesus' divinity, the New Testament writers make explicit parallels between Jesus and various Old Testament texts and prophecies that apply to Yahweh. Here are a few of many such examples:

Ps. 16:8-11 – "I keep the Lord always before me; with the Lord at my right, I shall never be shaken…" See Acts 2:25-28.

Ps. 68:19 – "You went up to its lofty height; you took captives, received slaves as tribute…" See Eph. 4:8.

Joel 3:5 – "Then everyone shall be rescued who calls on the name of the Lord…" See Rom. 10:13.

Is. 6:10 – "You are to make the heart of this people sluggish, to dull their ears and close their eyes; else their eyes will see, their ears hear, their heart understand, and they will turn and be healed." See Jn. 12:40.

Is. 45:23 – "To me every knee shall bend; by me every tongue shall swear..." See Phil. 2:10-11.

Deut. 10:17 – "For the Lord, your God, is God of gods, the Lord of lords, the great God, mighty and awesome..." See Rev. 17:14, 19:16.

If the Jehovah's Witnesses are correct about Jesus' nature—and he is not actually God at all, but only a creature—then not only would his death not be redemptive (since only God could pay the price for mankind's covenantal curse), but the high priests would have actually been quite correct in calling for his execution. For if he is not God, then he was an impious blasphemer who got precisely what he deserved.

THE HOLY TRINITY

Jesus draws a clear distinction between himself and the Father. Indeed, he refers to himself and the Father in the plural, as "we." He is equally definite about the Holy Spirit, the Advocate, whom he promised to send to guide us.

Jn. 14:23 – "Jesus answered and said to him, 'Whoever loves me will keep my word, and my Father will love him, and we will come to him and make our dwelling with him. Whoever does not love me does not keep my words; yet the word you hear is not mine but that of the Father who sent me.'" Jesus here distinguishes between himself and the Father by using the pronoun, "we." Some claim that the Father and Son are just different forms—or different roles—occupied by the same single being who is God. If this were so, it would make no sense for Jesus to refer to himself and the Father together as "we." I would never think of referring to myself in my various roles—as U.S. citizen, as father and as employee, say—as "we." There is no clearer evidence possible for the Trinity than this simple pronoun in the mouth of Jesus.

Jn. 17:3 – Jesus' prayer reveals the distinction between Father and Son: "Now this is eternal life, that they should know you, the only true God, and the one whom you sent, Jesus Christ. I glorified you on earth by accomplishing the work that you gave me to do. Now glorify me, Father, with you, with the glory that I had with you before the world began." Jesus and the Father shared in glory even before Creation; there is a clear distinction expressed here.

Jn. 14:25-26 – "I have told you this while I am with you. The Advocate, the Holy Spirit that the Father will send in my name—he will teach you everything and remind you of all that [I] told you." In this passage, Jesus is referring to the entire Holy Trinity—Father, Son and Holy Spirit. And the distinctions he makes between the three Persons are quite definite. The Father sends. The Son comes to earth. The Spirit teaches and inspires. The core theology of the Trinity is present in this one brief passage.

Jn. 6:44 – "No one can come to me unless the Father who sent me draw him, and I will raise him on the last day." Who but God can raise the dead? Even the Old Testament prophets who raised the dead prayed for God to act through them. Yet here Jesus says that *he*, not the Father, will raise the dead. And in the case of Lazarus of Bethany, Jesus himself commanded Lazarus to "come out." He did not call upon Yahweh here, or in any of his other miracles. In every case, he was acting on his own authority—which is not that of creature, but of Creator.

Rom. 8:14 – "For those who are led by the Spirit of God are children of God."

Acts 2:3-4 – "Then there appeared to them tongues as of fire, which parted and came to rest on each one of them. And they were all filled with the Holy Spirit and began to speak in different tongues, as the Spirit enabled them to proclaim." The Holy Spirit is an active agent of inspiration and change, not simply an attitude or a reflection. He is key to the establishment of the Church on that first Pentecost. Without the Holy Spirit, the apostles would have never had the power or the perseverance to carry out their mission.

Mt. 3:16-17 – "After Jesus was baptized, he came up from the water and behold, the heavens were opened [for him], and he saw the Spirit of God descending like a dove [and] coming upon him. And a voice came from the heavens, saying, 'This is my beloved Son, with whom I am well pleased.'" This is a clear reference to the Holy Trinity. Each of the divine Persons is described in vivid terms. Each is present, and together they act in perfect concert.

Acts 8:14-17 – When they were baptized in Jesus' name alone, the Samaritans did not receive the Holy Spirit. This indicates a clear differentiation between the Person of Jesus and the Holy Spirit: "Now when the apostles in Jerusalem heard that Samaria had accepted the word of God, they sent them Peter and John, who went down and prayed for them, that they might receive the Holy Spirit, for it had not yet fallen upon any of them; they had only been baptized in the name of the Lord Jesus. Then they laid hands on them and they received the Holy Spirit."

Some teach that Jesus was not God at all, but an archangel. This teaching is based, as so many errors are, on a few scripture passages taken out of context, and it dates back to the early centuries of the Church. Of course this position ignores another entire set of scripture verses which contradict the idea most decisively.

Heb. 1:5-13 – "For to which of the angels did God ever say: 'You are my son; this day I have begotten you'? Or again: 'I will be a father to him, and he shall be a son to me'? And again, when he leads the first-born into the world, he says: 'Let all the angels of God worship him.' Of the angels he says: 'He makes his angels winds and his ministers a fiery flame;' but of the son: 'Your throne, O God, stands forever and ever; and a righteous scepter is the scepter of your kingdom.' …to which of the angels has he ever said: 'Sit at my right hand until I make your enemies your footstool'? Are they not all ministering spirits sent to serve, for the sake of those who are to inherit salvation?" This passage is an altogether explicit response to the ancient heresy that Jesus was merely an angel. The author is addressing the issue head-on and showing its error.

Dan. 10:13 – "…Finally Michael, one of the chief princes, came to help me." Michael is only "one" of many. John 1, of course, tells us that Jesus is alone and unique, "the Word" of God through whom all of creation—including the heavenly hosts—came to be.

Jude 1:9 – "Yet the archangel Michael, when he argued with the devil in a dispute over the body of Moses, did not venture to pronounce a reviling judgment upon him but said, 'May the Lord rebuke you!'" Michael refers judgment to God. But unless he is quoting scripture, Jesus himself never addresses God directly with the term "Lord" for that is a word we creatures use to address our Creator and Master. But Jesus is not a creature; he himself *is* in fact "Lord."

Col. 1:16 – "For in him were created all things in heaven and on earth, the visible and the invisible, whether thrones or dominations or principalities or powers; all things were created through him and for him. He is before all things." Angels, too—including Lucifer himself— were created through the Son.

Col. 2:18 – "Let no one disqualify you, delighting in self-abasement and worship of angels, taking his stand on visions, inflated without reason by his fleshly mind, and not holding closely to the head, from whom the whole body, supported and held together by its ligaments and bonds, achieves the growth that comes from God." We are created to adore

God. Jesus, being God, is the object of our adoration. But in this passage, St. Paul clearly forbids the adoration of angels. So if Jesus were an angel, we would be forbidden to adore him—a clear contradiction of 1 Pet. 4:11, where we find, "…in all things God may be glorified through Jesus Christ, to whom belong glory and dominion forever and ever."

1 Thess. 4:16 – "For the Lord himself, with a word of command, with the voice of an archangel and with the trumpet of God, will come down from heaven, and the dead in Christ will rise first." This is one of the primary texts used by those who claim Jesus is an archangel. However, if Jesus were really an archangel, then "the voice of an archangel" would be the last phrase St. Paul would think of using to describe the sound of Jesus' voice. For who would ever describe the sound of an attacking lion with the sentence, "The vicious beast came at me with the roar of a lion"? If the Lord himself *is* an archangel, then what sense would it make to point out that he has the *voice* of an archangel?

Rev. 19:10 – "I fell at his feet to worship him. But he said to me, 'Don't! I am a fellow servant of yours and of your brothers who bear witness to Jesus. Worship God.'" The angel here makes a major distinction between himself and God. He, an angel, is not worthy of worship. Yet the scriptures tell us that our Lord Jesus Christ is in fact worthy of our adoration: "…in all things God may be glorified through Jesus Christ, to whom belong glory and dominion forever and ever." (1 Pet. 4:11.) *See also the above section, "The Divinity of Jesus."*

MARY, THE MOTHER OF GOD
MARY AS THE ARK OF THE NEW COVENANT

Catholics do not adore Mary, for the simple reason that she is not God. Indeed, some members of the early Christian community who actually did worship Mary—for example, the Collrydians who offered sacrifices to her—have in fact been excommunicated from the Church. No one who adores Mary can be a Catholic. Yes, we do certainly love Mary, and we are grateful to God for the gift she represents to humanity. For it was through Mary—quite literally—that salvation came into the world. She is shown by scripture to be the ark of the new covenant. As such, she is due greater esteem than the old ark, which was viewed by the ancient Israelites as the most precious and revered object in creation apart from the Creator himself. So we see that treating her as "just another Christian" is unbiblical, since even an angel of God pays homage to her in a remarkable and unprecedented manner, praising her as one would a royal personage (Lk. 1:28). In truth, when we venerate Mary we are fulfilling her clear New Testament prophecy:

Lk. 1:48 – "...Behold, from now on will all ages call me blessed." For two thousand years now, Mary's prophecy has been in a state of constant fulfillment.

Lk. 1:43 – Elizabeth's greeting, "...how does this happen to me, that the mother of my Lord should come to me?" isn't just unusual, it is absolutely radical. Elizabeth was "well advanced in years," far older than Mary. For her to address a younger relative in this way would have been completely unheard of in a culture with such rigidly hierarchical family customs. Further, Elizabeth's greeting clearly establishes Mary as the new ark of the covenant, since the phrase Elizabeth uses refers to the following Old Testament verse:

2 Sam. 6:9 – David asks, "How can the ark of the Lord come to me?" This passage parallels Elizabeth's greeting in Lk. 1:43 (above). Thus, Mary is shown to be the new ark of the covenant, the bearer of God, or *Theotokos*. When David, in fear, sent the ark to the house of Obededom, it stayed there three months (2 Sam. 6:11). Mary remained with Elizabeth for the same period of time—three months (Lk. 1:56). These parallels, which the New Testament writers knew would be obvious to the early Christian community which was steeped in the Old Testament scriptures, are not mere coincidences.

Rev. 11:19 - 12:1 – The ark of the covenant, described as being visible in the sanctuary of Heaven, refers to Mary, who is the new ark, being present there in body. For heaven is about perfected New Testament fulfillments, not imperfect Old Testament types: "Then God's temple in heaven was opened, and the ark of his covenant could be seen in the temple... A great sign appeared in the sky, a woman clothed with the sun, with the moon under her feet, and on her head a crown of twelve stars." The Ark of the Covenant parallels this queenly personage who can only be Mary, since her offspring is said to be "...destined to rule all the nations with an iron rod" (12:5). Note that the division of the Bible into chapters was not undertaken until the thirteenth century (*Where We Got The Bible*, Henry Graham, TAN Books, p. 58). So the separation between chapters 11 and 12 is an arbitrary device. To get an accurate understanding of John's words, we should read the verses as a unified whole.

Ps. 138:2 – "I bow low toward your holy temple..." How much more appropriate to bow toward the living temple of Jesus' own loving mother, within whom dwelled God-among-us, in both Body and Spirit.

Lev. 19:30 – "...Reverence my sanctuary. I am the Lord." Again, which is the greater sanctuary, a temple of stone, or the womb which actually sustained the God-man and gave him life? We are commanded to reverence the stone; then how can we then fail to reverence the woman through whom our Savior received his existence as a man, and who nurtured him, taught him, and loved him?

Lk. 1:35 – Gabriel tells Mary: "The Holy Spirit will come upon you, and the power of the Most High will overshadow you." The Greek word for "overshadow" is *epischiadze*, which is the same word used in reference to the Ark of the Covenant in the following passage. There it is translated as "settled down upon." Thus, once again, Mary is shown to be the new ark:

Ex. 40:34-35 – "The cloud covered the meeting tent, and the glory of the Lord filled the Dwelling. Moses could not enter the meeting tent because the cloud settled down upon it and the glory of the Lord filled the Dwelling." This verse clearly parallels Lk. 1:35 (above), since the unusual and very specific verb form *epischiadze* is used. Mary is associated with the old ark to show she is the ark of the new covenant. Since she is the fulfillment of the old ark, Mary is due all the homage paid to the old ark, and more. Also, just as Moses could not enter the Dwelling while the Spirit of the Lord was within, so no mere man could "enter" Mary. Such a thing would have been an unimaginable defilement.

Lk. 1:38 – Mary's assent was required before God would fulfill his Word. Think about this for a moment: God deigns to ask a humble human being's permission before he redeems the world. Also think about this: She had the power to say no. Of course, she does not say no. Instead, she utters her beautiful *fiat*, which is an exquisite one-phrase summation of the ultimate meaning of faith: "May it be done to me according to your word." The initiation of our redemption can be traced to Mary's assent, for this is the moment that signaled Christ's entrance into humanity. And the ark fulfilled its purpose.

Lk. 1:42 – Elizabeth, filled with the Holy Spirit, makes this radical, almost blasphemous statement: "Most blessed are you among women, and blessed is the fruit of your womb." She applies the same word, "blessed," both to I AM, the divine Creator of the universe, and to a mortal human creature, Mary. And, just as surprising, she actually pays homage to Mary *first*. In a culture so steeped in hierarchy and position, and so sensitive to desecration, this cannot have been an accident, either of St. Elizabeth's, of the Holy Spirit's, or of St. Luke's. This is not, of course, blasphemy, but a measure of the tremendous love and esteem in which the Holy Spirit holds his beloved spouse.

Please note: For some of the passages in the Marian sections of this book, the Douay-Rheims translation of the Bible is used. The Douay-Rheims version is more literal than our contemporary translations, so it captures nuances of the writers' intentions that broader translations do not. Incidentally, the Douay-Rheims Bible was one of those consulted by the translators of the original King James Bible. The two versions actually have much in common.

MARY AS THE NEW EVE

Judg. 5:24 – "Blessed among women be Jahel..." Mary is twice described as being "blessed among women"—once by Gabriel, in Lk. 1:28, and again by Elizabeth, in Lk. 1:42. Their words are a reference to this Old Testament verse which describes an incident in which Jahel, a woman of Israel, entices the leader of the opposing army into her tent, lulls him to sleep, then pierces his skull by pounding a tent peg into it. This reference to Jahel speaks of the fulfillment of the following divine prophecy:

Gen. 3:15 – "I will put enmities between thee and the woman, and thy seed and her seed: she shall crush thy head, and thou shalt lie in wait for her heel." The Hebrew pronoun is indefinite as to gender. The passage could be translated "she shall crush," referring to Mary, or "he shall crush," referring to Jesus. Jerome, in translating his Latin Vulgate, used the form, "she." Most modern translators use "he." However, even the fact that it is not definite is of interest. Luke's dual references to Jahel make his intention clear. Mary is the fulfillment of the Genesis prophecy. Like Jahel, Mary has crushed the head of evil. The "enmity" between Mary and Satan becomes all too clear in Revelation 12: "And the serpent cast out of his mouth after the woman, water as if it were a river, that he might cause her to be carried away by the river... And the dragon was angry against the woman..." (verses 15, 17). Eve and Jahel are types, and Mary is their fulfillment. All of these astonishing passages of the Old Testament are reconciled and fulfilled, St. Luke is telling us, in the person of Mary.

Jn. 2:3-4 – Jesus refers to his mother with the word for "woman," rendered in the Greek Septuagint as "gune," a term of high rank. Some feel that Jesus is admonishing his mother by using this word: "Woman, how does your concern affect me? My hour has not yet come." However, we know that Jesus could not have possibly been so disrespectful as to admonish his mother in public. That would have been a sin punishable by stoning. No, the term "gune" was a title of honor, for it is the same word that was used by God in his speech to Eve in Gen. 3:15 (see above).

Jn. 19:26 – Greek word "gune" as above, again used in reference to Mary. Clearly, the word "woman" in scripture is hardly a rebuke, however it may sound to modern ears.

Gal. 4:4 – Greek word "gune" as above, used to show great honor to Mary: "…when the fullness of time had come, God sent his Son, born of a woman, born under the law…"

DEVOTION TO MARY

As we saw in the previous section, the scripture writers are clear about the status of Mary: She is the queen who stands at the right hand of the Messiah; she is the ark of the new covenant, for her body held the Person of Jesus Christ. In a unique and marvelous way, she was the Dwelling of the Lord, his sanctuary. Now, if the old ark was the archetype of the new ark, we need only examine the way the Israelites regarded the old ark to discern how we should view the new ark.

1 Chron. 16:4 – "He (David) now appointed certain Levites to minister before the ark of the Lord, to celebrate, thank, and praise the Lord, the God of Israel." Priests "ministered before" the ark, showing it a special reverence. And it was a mere object. Mary is far more deserving of our veneration.

1 Chron. 16:37-38 – "Then David left Asaph and his brethren there before the ark of the covenant of the Lord to minister before the ark regularly according to the daily ritual; as he also left there Obed-edom and sixty-eight of his brethren, including Obed-edom, son of Jeduthum, and Hosah, to be gatekeepers." More than seventy people were specially assigned to "minister before" and protect the ark—an impressive display of devotion.

1 Chron. 29:20 – "…David besought the whole assembly, 'Now bless the Lord your God!' And the whole assembly blessed the Lord, the God of their fathers, bowing down and prostrating themselves before the Lord and before the king." Those who bow while addressing Mary are simply bowing down and prostrating themselves before the Lord and before the queen.

Lk. 1:28 – Gabriel praises Mary: "Hail, full of grace, the Lord is with thee: blessed art thou among women." This is a royal greeting. The Vulgate's salutation, "Ave," was the word used to greet Caesar, as in "Hail, Caesar!" It was also the word which the soldiers used to mock our Lord before his crucifixion. Of course to give their cruelty the greatest sting, they would have been sure to use the term of highest praise. "Kecaritomene," the Greek word translated as "full of grace," is actually a verb construction meaning "one who has been perfected in grace." Nowhere else in scripture does an angel pay homage to a human in this way. Indeed, in Rev. 19:10, even the great apostle John falls on his face in adoration before an angel because he is so overwhelmed by its presence: "I fell at his feet to worship him. But he said to me, 'Don't! I am a fellow servant of yours...'" And John repeats the same blunder just three chapters later, in Rev. 22:8, and has to be corrected again by the angel. Incredibly, Mary, a young and simple country girl, makes no such mistake. Instead, the angel is the one who pays homage to her—homage that reflects her status as Queen Mother to our Lord! This is more than astonishing—it is unparalleled in salvation history. (See the passage that follows.)

1 **Kings 2:13-25** – In ancient Middle Eastern kingdoms, the kings had many wives. So the person who assumed the role of queen was actually the queen mother—the king's own mother. In this passage, we see Solomon the king paying homage to his mother, Bathsheba. In fact he himself acknowledges that he cannot refuse her requests: "Then Bathsheba went to King Solomon to speak to him for Adonijah, and the king stood up to meet her and paid her homage. Then he sat down upon his throne, and a throne was provided for the king's mother, who sat at his right. 'There is one small favor I would ask of you,' she said. 'Do not refuse me.' 'Ask it, my mother,' the king said to her, 'for I will not refuse you.'" This is a striking image of the place of the royal mother. The king pays her homage at her appearance. He provides her with a throne. And she is seated at his right side, a vivid demonstration of her place and her power. And the king approves her request even before it is expressed. Another interesting note: on this occasion Bathsheba is in fact lobbying for Solomon's enemy and rival, Adonijah, who has tricked her. But even knowing this, the king cannot refuse his mother. Indeed, rather than deny her request, Solomon instead has Adonijah killed— his only way out of the situation. Would Jesus, the fulfillment of all royalty in salvation history, treat his own mother with less respect than the flawed Solomon showed Bathsheba—even to the point of offering her a throne? And if Jesus accords Mary this level of honor, acknowledging her as Queen of Heaven (see above, Rev. 11:19-12:1, in *Mary as Ark of the New Covenant*), then how could we ever honor her less—we who are infinitely less worthy than our Lord?

2 **Kings 11:1-3** – We see that the King's mother actually ruled in the king's place after he died, until the succession was established.

Ps. 138:2 – "I bow low toward your holy temple; I praise your name for your fidelity and love. For you have exalted over all your name and your promise." We are instructed to "bow low" before the temple, which contains the old ark. How much more ought we reverence the new ark herself. Thus we see that "bowing down" before Mary is not only acceptable, it is expected of those who are subject to the new covenant— that is, Christians. In other words, if we were to refuse to venerate Mary, it would be as if the Israelites, in professing their love of Yahweh, nonetheless refused to pay homage to the Dwelling of the Lord. But of course, such a thing would have been totally unthinkable.

Lev. 19:30 – "Keep my sabbaths, and reverence my sanctuary. I am the Lord." Mary is the sanctuary of the Lord in a sense far truer and far more intimate than Solomon's temple ever was. It was through Mary that Jesus received his human nature and it was through her that he was sustained in his human life. So to reverence Mary is entirely scriptural.

Ps. 134:2 – "Lift up your hands toward the sanctuary, and bless the Lord." We are directed to take a worshipful posture before the "sanctuary"— i.e., before Mary. Also, we see that when we bless Mary— "the sanctuary"—we are in reality blessing the Lord. This fact is key to understanding Catholics' devotion to Mary.

Gen. 27:29 – "Let peoples serve you and nations pay you homage." Here Isaac is saying that his son, Jacob, is deserving of the praise and homage of entire nations. How much more worthy is Mary, who carried God himself in her womb, who nourished him from her own body, who taught him to walk and talk and live according to the law.

Gen. 49:8 – "You, Judah, shall your brothers praise—your hand on the neck of your enemies, the sons of your father shall bow down to you." Jacob's prophecy about his son, Judah, includes his brothers bowing down before him. Since this is an occasion of great praise, it can in no way be offensive to God. Judah's brothers are not prostrating themselves in adoration, but are instead showing him the reverence he deserves. And how much more deserving of our reverence is Jesus' holy Mother, who carried God in her womb in a far closer and more intimate fashion than the ark of the covenant carried God's tablets. Yet God demanded such profound reverence for the ark that the slightest unauthorized touch was punished by death.

Gen. 33:3 – When Jacob was reunited with Esau, he "went on ahead of them, bowing to the ground seven times, until he reached his brother." There is no indication that Jacob's homage to his brother—bowing seven times—is at all offensive to God. So how can it be offensive to God when we bow to Mary, who is far more worthy of our veneration than Esau?

Josh. 5:13-15 – "While Joshua was near Jericho, he raised his eyes and saw one who stood facing him, drawn sword in hand. Joshua went up to him and asked, 'Are you one of us or of our enemies?' He replied, 'Neither. I am the captain of the host of the Lord, and I have just arrived.' Then Joshua fell prostrate to the ground in worship, and said to him, 'What has my lord to say to his servant?' The captain of the host of the Lord replied to Joshua, 'Remove your sandals from your feet, for the place on which you are standing is holy.' And Joshua obeyed." Some non-Catholic Christians are at times scandalized by the honor Catholics extend to Mary, including old texts and translations which use the word, "worship" in reference to her. However, the meaning of the word "worship" has changed. To our modern ears, it denotes adoration, which all Christians agree must be given to God alone, and not to any of his creatures. However, only a hundred years or so ago, "worship" meant "honor" and "respect"—as in the title, "your worship," a term found in English literature of the 19th century. Commoners use it as an honorific in addressing their social superiors. The point is, Joshua was not offering adoration to the angel, nor are Catholics who invoke Mary's intercession adoring her. The Church has always taught that Mary is a creature.

1 Sam. 28:14 – King Saul bows down to the spirit of the deceased Samuel: "...he bowed face to the ground in homage." Note that the holy prophet Samuel does not rebuke him for this action, so we must conclude that bowing to Samuel was not offensive to God.

Lk. 2:51 – "He went down with them and came to Nazareth, and was obedient to them." Mary delays the initiation of Jesus' ministry. Although still a boy, he was in the process of revealing himself to the temple elders through his masterful and authoritative interpretation of the scriptures (v. 47). However, at Mary's direction he left the temple and returned home with Mary and Joseph. (Also see passage below.)

Jn. 2:4 – "Jesus said to her, '...My hour has not yet come.'" Yet he accedes to her request that he reveal himself by turning the water to wine. Thus, Mary determines when Jesus' ministry actually begins. (See passage above.)

Jn. 19:26-30 – Mary also shares in the end of Jesus' ministry. His final act before dying is to place John into her care: "'Woman, behold your son.' Then he said to the disciple, 'Behold your mother.'" Then, "...aware that everything was finished..." he gave up his spirit.

Rev. 12:17 – Mary is referred to as the mother of all the faithful: "...her offspring, those who keep God's commandments and bear witness to Jesus." This passage reaffirms the fact that from the cross Jesus gave his mother to all of us, not only to the apostle John (Jn. 19:26-30, above).

Lk. 2:34-35 – The prophet Simeon definitively ties Jesus' suffering—and his revelatory power—to Mary: "Behold, this child is destined for the fall and rise of many in Israel, and to be a sign that will be contradicted (and you yourself a sword will pierce) so that the thoughts of many hearts may be revealed."

Ps. 45:7-18 – In this exquisite Messianic prophecy, we see a queen standing at the right hand of the Anointed One. This mysterious woman can only be Mary: "Your throne, O god, stands forever; your royal scepter is a scepter for justice... a princess arrayed in Ophir's gold comes to stand at your right hand... In embroidered apparel she is led to the king... I will make your name renowned through all generations; thus nations shall praise you forever." We know this prophecy refers to Mary, if only because in her Magnificat (Lk. 1:48, cited in the first verse above), the Evangelist has Mary herself proclaiming: "...behold, from now on will all ages call me blessed." Again, this reference cannot be a mistake. Luke is letting us know, in terms that any Jew of his day would have instantly recognized, that Mary is the fulfillment of this beautiful prophecy of the princess arrayed in gold.

1 Sam. 4:22 – "Gone is the glory from Israel." Eli's daughter-in-law makes this astonishing statement after the army of the Israelites is defeated, and the ark of the covenant is captured by the Philistines. Note that the glory of God departed when the ark was captured. To our minds, this sounds strange. God is everywhere, isn't he? And isn't God himself the glory of Israel rather than just the box containing the tablets, the staff that budded and the manna? Wouldn't all this fuss about a golden box detract from the people's devotion to God? Obviously not. God, in his mysterious and inscrutable way, gave himself to the nation through the ark. He used the ark to display his power and his Presence. When the ark was taken, Israel's glory was gone. This is the mystery and majesty of the Incarnation: That physical existence—including our own humanity—has real and tangible meaning. Thus, reality is not a mere reflection or illusion, as Buddhism propounds, but it is the arena where the struggle between good and evil takes place, where eternal souls are either lost or saved. It is here that we praise Immanuel— "God with us"—that is, God sharing our physical reality. And Mary was the first

Tabernacle of that awesome reality. Mary, as the new and living ark, is glorious in ways the old ark—the precursor—could never be. In a real and marvelous sense, Mary is the glory of the new Israel, the covenant sealed between God and man through the saving blood of her divine Son. The fact that a person—a creature—could be honored by God in this way is an awesome gift to each one of us.

MARY'S IMMACULATE CONCEPTION

The Immaculate Conception refers to the birth of Mary without original sin. Like the term, "Holy Trinity," the words, "Immaculate Conception," are not found in the Bible. But the foundation for the teaching most certainly is.

Ex. 25:8-16 – "They shall make a sanctuary for me, that I may dwell in their midst. This Dwelling and all its furnishings you shall make exactly according to the pattern that I will now show you." The old ark was prepared with great care, using all virgin materials, at the express and detailed direction of the Lord. As we saw above, Mary is the new ark; would she have been prepared with less care by God himself? Such a thing would be unthinkable.

Gen. 1:27 – "God created man in his image, in the divine image he created him; male and female he created them." Eve, the Old Testament archetype, was created without original sin; so too Mary, who is the New Testament fulfillment of Eve and who therefore is far greater than Eve, must have been created without original sin as well. It is not possible that the fulfillment would have been created lesser than the archetype. Nor is it possible that the new ark that would give life to the Immanuel would have been besmirched with sin, when the ark of the old covenant was created with perfect care and pristine materials.

Lk. 1:28 – Gabriel praises Mary: "Hail, full of grace, the Lord is with thee: blessed art thou among women." The Greek word translated as "full of grace" is actually a grammatical construction meaning "one who has been perfected in grace." Nowhere else does an angel honor a human in this way. Gabriel could not have used these words if Mary had been touched by sin.

Lk. 1:49 – "The Mighty One has done great things for me..." Mary makes the point that she has received wonderful and unique blessings from God. She does not say, "for us," or, "for all of humanity," but instead sets herself apart.

Rev. 21:27 – "...Nothing unclean will enter it [heaven], nor any [one] who does abominable things or tells lies." Anyone who thinks that Jesus could have been formed within—and by—a sinful person is misconstruing the nature of God and the nature of sin. God simply cannot be in communion with sin, which is why no one sinful can enter into heaven.

Rom. 3:10-18 – This is the primary proof-text of those who say Mary—along with the rest of humanity—was born in sin: "There is no one just, not one, there is no one who understands, there is no one who seeks God. All have gone astray; all alike are worthless; there is not one who does good, [there is not] even one. Their throats are open graves, they deceive with their tongues; the venom of asps is on their lips..." Those who claim this passage proves that everyone—inclucing Mary—is a sinner would seem to have a point, at least from a cursory reading. However there are two major problems with the universalist interpretation of this text. First, if this passage is to be taken literally, then we must conclude that Jesus himself was a sinner. For he at least is "one" who understands and seeks God; yet the text says there is "not one." Second, in this passage St. Paul is quoting Psalms 14 and 53. In Ps. 14, we read: "...not one does what is right. The Lord looks down from heaven upon the human race, to see if even one is wise, if even one seeks God. All have gone astray; all alike are perverse. Not one does what is right, not even one. Will these evildoers never learn? They devour my people as they devour bread... They would crush the hopes of the poor, but the poor have the Lord as their refuge." So we see the passage cannot be taken as meaning that every human being created since the time of Adam and Eve has been totally depraved, as the Reformers taught. For the psalmist is talking about "evildoers" who prey upon the people of God, "They prey upon my people as they devour bread." Clearly, these passages are condemning specific miscreants who are persecuting the just people of God. For St. Paul to misrepresent the meaning of the ancient texts he was quoting—and say they intended something that in their original context they clearly do not—would mean he is distorting the scriptures, which would be an absurdity.

MARY'S VIRGINITY (SEE ALSO "THE 'BROTHERS' OF JESUS" SECTION BELOW)

Jn. 19:27 – From the cross, Jesus places Mary in John's charge; Jesus could not have done this if he'd had brothers. This gesture would have been highly disrespectful to them.

2 Sam. 6:6-7 – Uzzah was killed for simply touching the ark, even though he meant no harm; he only wanted to save it from tipping over. Mary is the new ark and spouse of the Holy Spirit. Joseph could not have defiled her without suffering the same punishment that was meted out to Uzzah.

Ex. 40:34-35 – "Then the cloud covered the meeting tent, and the glory of the Lord filled the Dwelling. Moses could not enter the meeting tent because the cloud settled down upon it and the glory of the Lord filled the Dwelling." If no one, not even Moses, could enter into the meeting tent; what man could have "entered" the new ark and lived?

1 Cor. 7:37-38 – "The one who stands firm in his resolve, however, who is not under compulsion but has power over his own will, and has made up his mind to keep his virgin, will be doing well. So then, the one who marries his virgin does well; the one who does not marry her will do better." To St. Paul, the celibate state is always preferable to the conjugal state for those who have the discipline to maintain it. For those who cannot, the conjugal state is preferable to a life of sin. It is hardly surprising that a woman of Mary's faith would have followed the path of greatest piety.

1 Cor. 7:29 – "I tell you, brothers, the time is running out. From now on, let those having wives act as not having them..."

Rev. 14:2-5 – "These are they who were not defiled with women; they are virgins and these are the ones who follow the Lamb wherever he goes. They have been ransomed as the first fruits of the human race for God and the Lamb. On their lips no deceit has been found; they are unblemished."

THE "BROTHERS" OF JESUS

Protestants dispute Mary's perpetual virginity because of this verse: "Is not this the carpenter, the son of Mary, the brother of James, and Joseph, and Jude, and Simon?" (Mk. 6:3). Seems pretty clear, right? However, this interpretation is an example of the danger of viewing the scriptures through the lens of our modern language and culture. Because, as any scripture scholar will attest, the Israelites commonly referred to cousins, fellow tribesmen, and men who were totally unrelated by blood as "brother."

1 Chron. 6:18-28 – This passage refers to two men, Heman and Asaph, as "brothers." Yet in their genealogies—both of which are fully chronicled here—we can see that they have different fathers, different grandfathers and different great-grandfathers. The only ancestor they share, many generations back, is the father of their tribe, Levi. So it is clear that at times the Israelites used the word "brother" to signify relationships of men who were neither "brothers" nor even "cousins" in modern parlance, but what we would call "tribesmen." This makes sense, of course, since in the Israelites' past a person's life and livelihood depended more upon the fortunes of the tribe than on those of his immediate family. Life was difficult enough that a nuclear family alone would have had little chance of surviving. Further, this regarding of fellow tribe members as "brothers" would have meant greater cohesiveness—and smoother relations—within the tribe. This use of the word "brother"—quite foreign to most modern-day Americans—is an excellent illustration of why we cannot impose our own assumptions about family, society and language upon the scriptures without seriously distorting their meaning. This is a big reason why relying on one's own understanding of the Bible as the ultimate authority of faith is so very dangerous.

2 Sam. 1:26 – "I grieve for you Jonathan, my brother!" Jonathan was Saul's son, no relation to David. This is another example of the usage of the word "brother" to denote a close, non-filial relationship.

1 Kings 9:13 – "Where are these cities you have given me, my brother?" Hiram refers to Solomon as "brother" when they are not even of the same nation. Hiram is king of Tyre.

Amos 1:9 – "Thus says the Lord: For three crimes of Tyre, and for four, I will not evoke my word; because they delivered whole groups captive to Edom, and did not remember the pact of brotherhood, I will send fire upon the wall of Tyre, to devour her castles." The political and military alliance forged by Solomon with Hiram (above) is referred to by God himself as a "brotherhood." So we see that allies of no blood relation were referred to as brothers, even by God.

1 Kings 20:32 – "'Your servant Ben-hadad pleads for his life,' they said. 'Is he still alive?' the king asked. 'He is my brother.'" Ahab calls Ben-hadad "brother," although they are not even of the same nation.

Mk. 6:3 – Most of the confusion regarding Mary's virginity stems from liberties taken with this verse: "Is not this the carpenter, the son of Mary, the brother of James, and Joseph, and Jude, and Simon? Are not also his sisters here with us?" It is interesting to note that this verse does not say "*a* son of Mary," or "*one* of the sons of Mary." Besides the misunderstanding of the meaning of the word "brother" the difficulty also stems from the fact that the mother of James and Joseph is also named Mary:

Mt. 27:55-56 – "And there were there many women afar off, who had followed Jesus from Galilee, ministering unto him: Among whom was Mary Magdalen, and Mary the mother of James and Joseph..." Clearly, however, this Mary is not Jesus' mother, since the evangelist would not

114

have failed to identify her as such on Calvary. This is evident as well in the following passage:

Mk. 15:40 – "And there were also women looking on afar off: among whom was Mary Magdalen, and Mary the mother of James the less and of Joseph... These women had followed him when he was in Galilee and ministered to him." Again, the fact that this Mary is not Jesus' mother is quite clear.

Lk. 6:15-16 – This passage which lists the names of the apostles clarifies the matter further, since "James the less," who is referred to in the passage above as the son of a certain Mary, is said to be "the son of Alpheus"— and *not* the son of Joseph.

Jn. 19:25 – The Evangelist John identifies this additional Mary at the cross as "...his mother's sister, Mary of Cleophas..." So apparently both Mary's—Jesus' mother and the mother of James and Joseph—were close blood relatives. This is an important clue about the Mk. 6:3 verse, above, which lists James and Joseph as Jesus' "brothers." Close blood relatives— including cousins and nephews—were frequently called "brothers," since the most important social unit was the tribe rather than the nuclear family. The male members of a tribe regarded all other males in the tribe as "brothers." And tribesmen always considered themselves descendents of the tribe's founder, even though that may not have been true, as happened in the case of individuals who were cast out of one tribe and joined another.

Mt. 10:2-4 – Neither of the apostles named James is a son of Joseph and Mary, so neither can be termed a "brother" of Jesus in the sense we use the term. James the elder is said to be the son of Zebedee, and James the younger the son of Alpheus. The Bible is very clear on this point: "And the names of the twelve apostles are these: The first, Simon who is called Peter, and Andrew his brother, James the son of Zebedee, and John his brother, Philip and Bartholomew, Thomas and Matthew the publican, and James the son of Alpheus, and Thaddaeus, Simon the Cananean, and Judas Iscariot, who also betrayed him."

Lk. 2:41-52 – In the account of the young Jesus being found by his parents in the temple in Jerusalem, no mention is made of siblings. By this time, Jesus was twelve years old. Chronologically, this is the latest mention of St. Joseph found in the gospels, yet we see no mention of other children.

Jn. 19:27 – From the cross, Jesus places Mary into the care of St. John. Jesus could not have done this if he'd had brothers. The gesture would have been highly disrespectful to them.

A remaining objection to this scenario is, of course, the question of why James and Joseph (Mt. 27:55-56, above) are identified as sons of Alpheus, while their mother is said to be the wife of Cleophas. Two possibilities exist: Either the mother of James and Joseph re-married Cleophas after the father of her sons died, or Alpheus and Cleophas were the same person—since men in Hebrew society were at times known by more than one name. Also, in ancient Israel, it was disrespectful for younger brothers to advise older brothers, but Jesus' "brothers" do advise him—most rudely, in fact (see verse below). So if Jesus had brothers by blood, they must have been older, or they never would have talked to him like this. But scripture is absolutely explicit that Jesus was in every sense firstborn. Therefore, he could not have had brothers by blood:

Jn. 7:3-4 – "So his brothers said to him, 'Leave here...'" In the highly structured and hierarchical society of the time, younger brothers could not have spoken so brusquely to an older sibling; they would have risked being stoned. Yet we know that if they were brothers in the modern sense, they could not have been older, since Jesus is referred to as the "first born" of Mary (Lk. 2:7).

Mk. 3:21 – "When his relatives heard of this they set out to seize him, for they said, 'He is out of his mind...'" These verses alone, in which his supposed "relatives" speak out harshly and publicly against Jesus, are alone enough to prove that there could not have been younger brothers among this group. In this society, younger brothers could never have treated an elder sibling with such contempt. They were most likely cousins or fellow tribesmen.

MARY'S "UNTIL"

Mary's virginity is most often attacked by citing Mt. 1:25, where we find this reference to Joseph and Mary: "He had no relations with her until she bore a son..." However, concluding that this passage implies that Joseph and Mary had relations after Jesus was born is a serious misinterpretation of the term "until" as it is used in the scriptures. In the Bible, the word "until" is often used in a specific way to imply only the fulfillment of certain conditions. It indicates nothing about what occurs after those conditions are fulfilled. Thus, the verse in question does not in any way imply that Joseph and Mary had relations after Jesus' birth. It only states that they did not up till that point. The following examples will doubtless help clarify the matter:

1 Cor. 15:25 – "..He must reign until he has put all his enemies under his feet." Clearly, Jesus reigns after that as well.

Mt. 28:18-20 – "...Behold, I am with you always, until the end of the age." Who would conclude from this that Jesus will no longer be with us after the end of the world? Yet we must hold to that interpretation if we also conclude that Joseph and Mary had relations after Jesus' birth.

2 **Sam 6:23** – "And so Saul's daughter Michal was childless to the day of her death." It is hardly likely that after her death she had children. However, we must make that assumption if we are to be consistent with the assumption that Joseph and Mary had relations after Jesus was born.

Deut. 34:6 – "Moses, the servant of the Lord, died as the Lord had said; and he was buried in the ravine opposite Beth-peor in the land of Moab, but to this day no one knows the place of his burial..." They still don't, of course, thousands of years after this verse was written.

1 **Mac. 5:53** – "...And Judas kept rounding up stragglers and encouraging the people the whole way, until he reached the land of Judah." It is hardly likely that such encouragement ceased after their arrival in the land of Judah.

Jn. 5:17 – "...Jesus answered them, 'My Father is at work until now, so I am at work.'" Did the Father stop working upon the birth of the Messiah?

MARY'S ASSUMPTION

While not specifically attested to in scripture, Mary's assumption is not in the least <u>contrary</u> to scripture, since we find several examples of biblical precedents for such occurrences.

Acts 2:27 – "...Because you will not abandon my soul to the nether world, nor will you suffer your holy one to see corruption." Refers to:

Ps. 16:10 – "...For you will not abandon me to Sheol, nor let your faithful servant see the pit." The body's eventual decay is caused by sin. The very holy are spared bodily corruption.

Gen. 5:24 – "Then Enoch walked with God, and he was no longer here, for God took him." Enoch was assumed, body and spirit, into heaven. So we see that such an occurrence has scriptural precedent.

Heb. 11:5 – "By faith Enoch was taken up so that he should not see death...he was attested to have pleased God." There is clear scriptural precedent for the idea that holy ones are taken into heaven, body and soul.

2 **Kings 2:1-13** – Elijah is taken bodily into heaven in a chariot. So the idea that another holy person would be taken bodily into heaven does not contradict the scriptures in the least. The scriptures never claimed to contain every saying and every event in the life of Jesus and the early Church. In fact we know they do not (Jn. 16:12-13; Jn. 21:25). Also, if Mary lived to old age—90 or 100 years—she could have outlived the

writing of the scriptures. So her assumption would have been impossible to record.

Ps. 132:8 – "Arise, Lord, come to your resting place, you and your majestic ark." The Old Testament resting place of God is the Dwelling within the temple sanctuary in Jerusalem. The New Testament fulfillment of Jerusalem, seen in Revelation, is heaven. The New Testament fulfillment of the temple is the sanctuary of heaven. Since the New Testament fulfillment of the ark, as we saw above, is Mary's body, we can conclude that Mary's body—as opposed to just her spirit—must be in heaven. Otherwise this passage of scripture would not be true.

Rev. 11:19 - 12:1 – The ark of the covenant is described by John as being visible in the sanctuary of Heaven. This is a clear reference to Mary, the ark of the new covenant, being present in body in the heavenly sanctuary. For heaven is about perfected New Testament fulfillments, not imperfect Old Testament types: "Then God's temple in heaven was opened, and the ark of his covenant could be seen in the temple... A great sign appeared in the sky, a woman clothed with the sun, with the moon under her feet, and on her head a crown of twelve stars." The ark of the covenant parallels this queenly personage who can only be Mary, since her offspring is said to be "...destined to rule all the nations with an iron rod" (12:5). Note that the separation between chapters is an arbitrary device that was not introduced until the thirteenth century. So we should read the above verses as a unit.

The early Church fathers recognized the parallel between Eve and Mary, upon which much of the Church's teachings about Mary are based. At the end of the second century—still more than 100 years before the canon of the New Testament was established—we find the great theologian, St. Irenaeus, writing: "Thus, the knot of Eve's disobedience was loosed by the obedience of Mary. What the virgin Eve had bound in unbelief, the Virgin Mary loosed through faith." (The Faith of the Early Fathers, Vol. 1, William A. Jurgens, [Collegeville, Minnesota: Liturgical Press, 1970] p. 93.)

NEW COVENANT FULFILLS OLD

The new covenant did not destroy the old; it fulfilled it. The Catholic Church looks at salvation history as a seamless garment. We are the children of Abraham, Isaac, Jacob and Moses. Our liturgies have much in common with those of our Jewish brethren. For example, no other Christian faith tradition enshrines the Holy Writ, processing in at the beginning of each Mass with the Bible held aloft. Yet our Jewish brethren do precisely that. The most ancient Christian tradition founded by Jesus and the apostles—in other words, the Catholic Christian faith—is in truth the faith of the Jews in the full blossom of its fulfillment.

2 Cor. 3:2-3 – "You are our letter, written on our hearts, known and read by all, shown to be a letter of Christ administered by us, written not in ink but by the Spirit of the living God, not on tablets of stone but on tablets that are hearts of flesh." The new covenant is living and vital, not legalistic and dead.

2 Cor. 3:7-9 – "Now if the ministry of death, carved in letters on stone, was so glorious that the Israelites could not look intently at the face of Moses because of its glory that was going to fade, how much more will the ministry of the Spirit be glorious?" This passage refers to Ex. 34:29-35. It clearly shows that the new covenant is more glorious than the old.

Heb. 8:13 – "When he speaks of a 'new' covenant, he declares the first one obsolete. And what has become obsolete and has grown old is close to disappearing." Since the new covenant has blossomed forth from the stump of the old, it is the new that we see bearing fruit. Yet they are both expressions of the same family of God—the old having been fulfilled by the new.

Heb. 9:23-28 – "Therefore, it was necessary for the copies of the heavenly things to be purified by these rites, but the heavenly things themselves by better sacrifices than these. For Christ did not enter into a sanctuary made by hands, a copy of the true one, but heaven itself, that he might now appear before God on our behalf." The old covenant prefigures the new.

Heb. 10:1 – The Old Testament types—prefigurements only—are fulfilled in New Testament truths: "Since the law has only a shadow of the good things to come, and not the very image of them..."

INTERPRETING SCRIPTURES

The Catholic Church treats scripture the way Jesus treated scripture. The Church knows that much of the truth in the Bible is hidden and is not easily or automatically grasped by all. Jesus himself had to open the truth of the scriptures for his followers before they could understand many of the passages that pertained to his life—even after most of them had been fulfilled. The Bible is actually a tremendously complex set of books, written over a span of many hundreds of years, by people with very different cultural backgrounds, different languages, and different world views. Certainly, the Holy Spirit inspired each of the Bible's authors. But that does not mean that the personality or the knowledge of each was overwhelmed by God or that the individual ceased to exist while he was writing. To ascertain the meaning of so much that is found in scripture, we must seek to understand the assumptions, the perspectives, the languages, and the customs of the authors. Only then can we begin to come to an appreciation of the depths of the books we know as the Bible. Which is why the Protestant doctrine of "sola scriptura"—whichever of the several different ways it can be defined—is hardly reassuring. Coming to a clear understanding of the scriptures is in fact an immensely daunting challenge, absolutely insurmountable to all but the most erudite scholars of scripture, ancient languages, and Jewish history and culture.

Lk. 24:13-35 – Jesus had to teach his disciples the meaning of the scriptures before they could understand. "Scripture alone" was not enough for them to grasp the truth: "Then beginning with Moses and all the prophets, he interpreted to them what referred to him in all the scriptures." Although they had access to the scriptures and had studied them all their lives, the disciples needed an authoritative interpretation of what they had read so many times before they could understand. Are we so different that we believe we can come to a full and complete understanding of these difficult passages on our own?

Acts 17:10-12 – "These Jews were more fair-minded than those in Thessalonica, for they received the word with all willingness and examined the scriptures daily to determine whether these things were so." This passage about the Beroeans is often the primary text used to support "sola scriptura." However, it actually supports the dual authority of Sacred Tradition and Scripture, since nowhere does it suggest that the Beroeans, without St. Paul's presence and without the help of his authoritative and apostolic oral teachings, could have ever concluded that Jesus of Nazareth was the Messiah. Indeed, they could not have. They were looking to the scriptures to see if what St. Paul said was contradicted there—and it is not. But there was no way they—or Nicodemus, or anyone else—could have come to the conclusion that Jesus is the Messiah by simply using "scripture alone." Even the man who was perhaps the greatest scripture scholar of all time, St. Paul, needed the help of direct divine revelation—being thrown to the ground, rendered blind and hearing the voice of Jesus—before he was able to grasp the truth. For, although St. Paul tells us he was thoroughly schooled in the scriptures (Phil. 3:5), we know that "scripture alone" was not enough to lead him to the simple fact that Jesus was the Messiah. Nor did the Holy Spirit enlighten him on this point when he sat and read the scriptures, as he had done so often as a Pharisee.

Eph. 3:8 – "To me, the very least of all the holy ones, this grace was given, to preach to the Gentiles the inscrutable riches of Christ, and to bring to light [for all] what is the plan of the mystery hidden from ages past in God who created all things." This is what Paul did for the Beroeans (Acts. 17:10-12); they needed Paul to teach them before they understood the hidden truths of the scriptures. The Spirit did not directly enlighten each individual.

1 Cor. 2:7-8 – God's truths are not instantly grasped by all; we need teachers like Paul to unlock them: "...we speak God's wisdom, mysterious, hidden, which God predetermined before the ages for our glory, and which none of the rulers of this age knew..."

1 Cor. 2:12-13 – "We have not received the spirit of the world but the Spirit that is from God, so that we may understand the things freely given us by God." Discernment of the truth—whether in the scriptures or elsewhere—is not easy or automatic. We have no guarantee from God that he will spontaneously grant every individual insight into the truths of the Bible.

Num. 11:27-29 – "...When a young man quickly told Moses, 'Eldad and Medad are prophesying in the camp,' Joshua, son of Nun, who from his youth had been Moses' aide, said, 'Moses, my lord, stop them.' But Moses answered him, 'Are you jealous for my sake? Would that all the people of the Lord were prophets! Would that the Lord might bestow his spirit on them all!'" But despite Moses' wish, the Lord has not bestowed his Spirit upon all, and all are not prophets. Yet this is the basis for the false doctrine of "sola scriptura," which states that the Holy Spirit will automatically lead all the faithful to the truth of the scriptures, or, in other words, that he will turn all into prophets.

Heb. 9:23-28 – "Therefore, it was necessary for the copies of the heavenly things to be purified by these rites, but the heavenly things themselves by better sacrifices than these. For Christ did not enter into a sanctuary made by hands, a copy of the true one, but heaven itself, that he might now appear before God on our behalf." Typology is specifically referred to here, and typology requires interpetation. It is not self-revealing.

Heb. 10:1 – "Since the law has only a shadow of the good things to come, and not the very image of them..." The Catholic Church views the scriptures—Old Testament and New—as a seamless garment. The personages, institutions and practices of the Old Testament prefigure and illuminate the New. The truth weaves the scriptures together until they are an infinite tapestry. It is not compartmentalized.

1 Pet. 3:20-21 – Another reference to typology: "…God patiently waited in the days of Noah during the building of the ark, in which a few persons, eight in all, were saved through water. This prefigured baptism, which saves you now." St. Peter is illustrating how the scriptures are a unified and tightly woven work. To fail to grasp this fact is to fail to perceive the profound depths of God's written word.

Jn. 3:14-15 – "And just as Moses lifted up the serpent in the desert, so must the Son of Man be lifted up, so that everyone who believes in him may have eternal life." Jesus himself uses typology to teach us the meaning of the scriptures. Here he is stating that he is the fulfillment of the bronze serpent, which Moses held up on a pole and which saved the Israelites from snakebite. The bronze serpent was the "type," or precursor, and Jesus is the fulfillment.

Acts 8:30-31 – The Holy Spirit does not infuse wisdom or knowledge of scripture to individuals simply through the act of picking up a book. We need an authoritative teacher to help us discern its truths: "Philip ran up and heard him reading Isaiah the prophet and said, 'Do you understand what you are reading?' He replied, 'How can I unless someone instructs me?'"

OUR ULTIMATE AUTHORITY NOT "SCRIPTURE ALONE"

The Protestant doctrine of "sola scriptura" is not really about scripture at all. It's about the claim that each person who picks up a Bible will be unerringly guided to the truth by the inspiration of the Holy Spirit. It is, in short, a claim of infallibility—not for one faithful and learned man sitting in Rome, who has been anointed by the authority which Christ bestowed upon his apostles, but for millions of individuals regardless of their education, their sensitivity, their knowledge of those who wrote the Bible or the forms of literature contained in it, their prayer life or their spirituality—or even the nature of their intentions. It is an exceedingly dangerous doctrine, since it leaves good and faithful Christians vulnerable to unscrupulous, unaccountable leaders. In the words of author Robert Sungenis, "Fallible men will invariably produce fallible interpretations of Scripture." Our Lord and Savior loves his flock too much to leave us under the dangerous influence of "false prophets, who come to you in sheep's clothing, but underneath are ravenous wolves." (Mt. 7:15.) Which is why he established his Church, directing Peter to tend his sheep (Jn. 21:16), and promising to send his Spirit to guide her leaders to all truth (Jn. 16:13).

2 Thess. 2:15 – "…Brothers, stand firm and hold fast to the traditions that you were taught, either by an oral statement or by a letter of ours."

St. Paul is exceedingly clear as he upholds both tradition and oral teaching and commands the faithful to preserve them. If "sola scriptura" were true, he would have been required to urge his readers to hold fast to scripture and to leave everything else behind. Of course nowhere does he—or any other apostle, or any Church Father—make any such statement. Thus, the principle of "sola scriptura" is self-negating. It states, in effect: "Scripture alone is the supreme authority in every principle of faith except this one, which is not found—or even hinted at—anywhere in the scriptures."

2 Thess. 3:6 – "We instruct you, brothers, in the name of [our] Lord Jesus Christ, to shun any brother who conducts himself in a disorderly way and not according to the tradition they received from us." Again, St. Paul expects his followers to acknowledge the authority of oral traditions, not just his letters. In fact, in every instance, his letters were written to support the teachings he had previously imparted verbally.

1 Cor. 11:2 – "I praise you because you remember me in everything and hold fast to the traditions, just as I handed them on to you." Apostolic tradition seems to be worth preserving, at least according to St. Paul.

Mt. 23:1 – In this single passage, Jesus himself acknowledges both the authority of tbe Church hierarchy and of oral tradition: "...Jesus spoke to the crowds and to his disciples, saying, 'The scribes and the Pharisees have taken their seat on the chair of Moses. Therefore, do and observe all things whatsoever they tell you, but do not follow their example.'" The uprightness of the Pharisees was not the basis of their authority, for with their hard hearts, they were hardly worthy of emulation. Instead, their authority derived from their position as the leaders of the community. Note also Jesus' use of the phrase, "chair of Moses." These words are not found in the Old Testament, so Jesus is himself adhering to the oral tradition of the Jews in presenting this teaching. It is clear that "sola scriptura" is not found in the Bible, either in word or in practice. We must conclude it is one of the traditions of men that St. Paul warns us against in Col. 2:8.

Acts 8:30-31 – Scripture itself tells us that it is in fact not self-revealing. The Holy Spirit does not infuse wisdom or knowledge of scripture to individuals simply through the act of picking up a book: "Philip ran up and heard him reading Isaiah the prophet and said, 'Do you understand what you are reading?' He replied, 'How can I unless someone instructs me?'"

Eph. 3:10 – St. Paul tells us the Church—not the scriptures—instructs even the angels: "...so that the manifold wisdom of God might now be made known through the church to the principalities and authorities in the heavens."

2 Tim. 3:16-17 – This is the passage most often cited by those trying to uphold the doctrine of "sola scriptura": "All scripture is inspired by God and is useful for teaching, for refutation, for correction, and for training in righteousness, so that one who belongs to God may be competent, equipped for every good work." However, here St. Paul is saying nothing about the scriptures as a source of spiritual authority, nor is he comparing the scriptures to other sources of spiritual authority. He is only saying the scriptures are very helpful in preparing believers for life in the spirit—which of course is not in dispute.

Jas. 1:4 – "And let perseverance be perfect, so that you may be perfect and complete, lacking in nothing." This verse balances 2 Tim. 3:16-17 (immediately above), which is usually cited as the primary proof of "sola scriptura." Does scripture make us complete and lacking in nothing, or does perseverance? Obviously, we cannot interpret these passages literally, or they would contradict one other.

1 Cor. 2:12-13 – In addition to his writings, St. Paul's speech is also inspired by the Holy Spirit when he speaks: "We have not received the spirit of the world but the Spirit that is from God, so that we may understand the things freely given us by God. And we speak about them not with words taught by human wisdom, but with words taught by the Spirit, describing spiritual realities in spiritual terms." Of course "sola scriptura" would have us ignore everything but the written form of revelation. If the Corinthians to whom St. Paul was writing had subscribed to "sola scriptura," they would have ignored his preaching and heeded only his letters. This would have been an obviously absurd approach for them to take. Yet it is the position "sola scriptura" adherents expect us to hold to today.

Acts 17:11 – "These Jews were more fair-minded than those in Thessalonica, for they received the word with all willingness and examined the scriptures daily to determine whether these things were so." This is probably the primary proof text used to support "sola scriptura." However, it actually supports the dual authority of Sacred Tradition and scripture, since nowhere does it suggest that these people, the Beroeans, could have ever concluded that Jesus of Nazareth was the Messiah without the oral teaching of St. Paul. Indeed, they could not have. When you think about it, there was one New Testament group that actually did cling to "scripture alone" and refused to believe the oral testimony of even Jesus himself—the Pharisees. They were the ones who sought to counter Jesus' influence with verse after verse of scripture. Yet the truth did not come to them through "scripture alone".

Eph. 3:8 – "To me, the very least of all the holy ones, this grace was given, to preach to the Gentiles the inscrutable riches of Christ, and to bring to light [for all] what is the plan of the mystery hidden from ages past in God who created all things." This is what St. Paul did for the Beroeans (Acts. 17:10-12); they needed Paul to teach them before they understood the hidden truths of the scriptures. The Spirit did not directly enlighten each individual. (See passage above.)

3 Jn. 13-14 – "I have much to write to you, but I do not wish to write with pen and ink. Instead, I hope to see you soon, when we can talk face to face." John equates the authority of the apostles' spoken word with the authority of the written word. They are one and the same.

2 Pet. 1:20 – "Know this first of all, that there is no prophecy of scripture that is a matter of personal interpretation..." Personal interpretation alone can lead us astray. We do not have the authority to come to a definitive interpretation of the scriptures on our own. And note the importance which St. Peter attaches to this truth— "know this first of all."

2 Pet. 3:16 – "...There are some things hard to understand that the ignorant and unstable distort to their own destruction, just as they do the other scriptures." The Bible may be misinterpreted, intentionally or not. God has given us no guarantee that our insights into the scriptures will be without error. And without an authoritative voice to interpret the scriptures, a voice that is guided by the Holy Spirit, discord will reign. This is what we see in the tens of thousands of Protestant denominations that exist in America today. While they all agree that the scriptures are their ultimate authority, no two denominations can agree on what the scriptures actually say. This tragic condition—which can result in a loss of faith as doctrinal disputes arise, leaders and teachings change, and groups within congregations are expected to keep pace or else break away—is not authored by the Holy Spirit.

1 Cor. 11:27-34 – "Therefore, my brothers, when you come together to eat, wait for one another. If anyone is hungry, he should eat at home, so that your meetings may not result in judgment. The other matters I shall set in order when I come." St. Paul is explicit: On this serious matter—the abuse of the Eucharist, which is actually resulting in the illness and death of some of the abusers—Paul says he has teachings he wishes to impart in person, apart from his written message. But the doctrine of "sola scriptura" would not have us consider those oral teachings inspired or binding.

Gal. 1:8 – "But even if we or an angel from heaven should preach to you a gospel other than the one that we preached to you, let that one be accursed!" Note that St. Paul is referring to the truth of the gospel having been "preached" to the faithful, not "written." Nowhere does he instruct believers to adhere to the gospel in written form.

2 Thess. 2:5 – In referring to the "lawless one," Paul refers to oral teachings and prophesies he made at an earlier date which he expects his readers to recall and to heed: "...do you not recall that while I was still with you I told you these things?" He expects his readers to consult his oral teachings in order to discern the truth. He intends his writings to support and reinforce his teaching and preaching, not simply to stand alone.

Lk. 24:13-35 – Jesus had to teach his disciples the meaning of the scriptures before they could understand. "Scripture alone" was not enough for them: "Then beginning with Moses and all the prophets, he interpreted to them what referred to him in all the scriptures." An aside: many believe that the Church's Sacred Tradition contains much of what the Lord imparted to his followers on the road to Emmaus—specifically the parallels between Adam and Jesus, Moses and Jesus, and the prophets and Jesus, not to mention the astonishing convergences of Calvary and Passover. Yet, since these are interpretations taught us by the early fathers, and not formally stated in scriptures, the more fundamentalist brands of "sola scriptura" would have us reject it.

Lk. 7:18-23 – Even John the Baptist, who was filled with the Holy Spirit from before his birth (Lk. 1:15), could not discern Jesus' true nature from "scripture alone." He sent his followers to query Jesus. And this is important: Jesus did not answer them with any direct claim. Instead, he interpreted the hidden truths in scriptures for them, "Go and tell John what you have seen and heard: the blind regain their sight, the lame walk, lepers are cleansed, the deaf hear, the dead are raised, the poor have the good news proclaimed to them." John's followers get no new information here. Only an authoritative interpretation of scriptures. If "sola scriptura" were true—that we need no authority to interpret scriptures for us—John and his followers would not have required this clarification from Jesus.

Jn. 5:39-40 – If "sola scriptura" were true, the Holy Spirit would have inspired the temple leaders to discern the fullness of truth through the scriptures which they so scrupulously searched. Instead, Jesus condemns them for relying on scripture alone: "You search the scriptures, because you think you have eternal life through them; even they testify on my behalf. But you do not want to come to me to have life." We know that the scriptures testify on behalf of Jesus. But the Pharisees, relying on "scripture alone," could not discern that truth. Indeed, not even Jesus' own followers could (Lk. 24:13-35). They needed Jesus to open the truth of the scriptures for them.

Jn. 16:12-13 – Jesus tells us he is not able to disclose "all truth" during his time on earth. He says he will send the Holy Spirit who is to come; this is a clear statement concerning inspired teaching and the deepening of our understanding of the faith: "I have much more to tell you, but you cannot bear it now. But when he comes, the Spirit of truth, he will guide you to all truth."

Eph. 3:3 – "...The mystery was made known to me by revelation, as I have written briefly earlier." St. Paul specifically states that he not fully imparted the entirety of his revelation through his writings. He also imparts them verbally. He intends his writings to support and reinforce his preaching, not to stand alone. Also, note that St. Paul did not come to faith in Christ Jesus through "scripture alone," but through revelation. Indeed, nowhere do we see a single person converted by reading the scriptures, nor do we see a single instance of any holy person appealing to the scriptures as their ultimate authority. Only Satan and the Pharisees and scribes do that, and in each instance it is in an attempt to trip up Jesus.

1 Tim. 3:15 – St. Paul says the foundation of truth is the Church, not the scriptures: "...Church of the living God, the pillar and foundation of truth." This is only logical, since it was the Church that declared which of the texts that were being read during Mass by the early believers were in fact inspired. So history shows us that the Bible rests on the authority of the Church, not vice versa.

Lk. 10:16 – "Whoever listens to you listens to me..." Jesus upholds oral teaching, telling his followers to go out and preach. In fact, Jesus never instructed his followers to write a single word.

1 Jn. 4:6 – "...Anyone who knows God listens to us, while anyone who does not belong to God refuses to hear us. This is how we know the spirit of truth and the spirit of deceit." Submitting to apostolic authority—not adherence to "scripture alone"—is the hallmark of the truth of our beliefs.

Heb. 13:17 – "Obey your leaders and defer to them, for they keep watch over you..." The writer urges believers to obedience, not to developing their own individual Bible interpretations, nor even to an exhaustive study of the ancient languages, cultures, and customs so that they might come to a more complete understanding of the scriptures. Those of us who are too busy with our daily responsibilities—jobs, families, etc.—to mount such a monumental scholastic undertaking need not worry. As long as we follow the teachings of our anointed leaders—and defer to them—we will not be led astray.

2 Tim. 2:2 – Nowhere does St. Paul teach "sola scriptura." On the contrary, we see him invoking apostolic succession. St. Paul is Jesus' near contemporary, and he is writing to the younger Timothy about sharing the Truth with the generations to come. But the written word is not mentioned: "So you, my child, be strong in the grace that is in Christ Jesus. And what you have heard from me through many witnesses entrust to faithful people who will have the ability to teach others as well." Timothy is explicitly instructed to preserve the oral teachings of St. Paul. Of course he did, as did his successors, and that is how the deposit of Sacred Tradition has been passed along to the present generation.

1 Thess. 2:13 – "And for this reason we too give thanks to God unceasingly, that, in receiving the word of God from hearing us, you received not a human word but, as it truly is, the word of God, which is now at work in you who believe." St. Paul is telling us his speech is as inspired and authoritative as his writings. The word is not static and limited to the page. It is dynamic—alive in the mind, on the lips, and in the heart of the Church he founded.

Rom. 10:14-15 – Again, we do not see St. Paul invoking the authority of the scripture, but the authority of those who preach: "And how can they hear without someone to preach? And how can people preach unless they are sent? As it is written, 'How beautiful are the feet of those who bring the good news!'" Those who brought the good news were speaking it out loud. In fact, most historians agree that this letter of Paul's was written before the gospels.

Deut. 19:15 – Scripture itself requires more than one witness to establish truth: "One witness alone shall not take the stand against a man in regard to any crime or any offense of which he may be guilty, a judicial fact shall be established on the testimony of two or three witnesses." Thus, the Hebrews would never have upheld the doctrine of "sola scriptura," for it asks us to trust the testimony of a single witness—the scripture alone.

Jn. 8:17 – Jesus affirms the fact that a single witness is not sufficient, even when that witness is Jesus himself: "Even in your law it is written that the testimony of two men can be verified. I testify on my behalf and so does the Father who sent me." Jesus did not expect even his own testimony to be accepted without corroboration by another – the Father.

Yet the Protestant position would have us look to a single witness only—that of scripture.

2 Cor. 13:1 – St. Paul reinforces the above passage: "This third time I am coming to you. 'On the testimony of two or three witnesses a fact shall be established.'" But the doctrine of "sola scriptura" would have us believe that a single witness—that of scripture—is sufficient.

Eph. 4:11-16 – "And he gave some as apostles, others as prophets, others as evangelists, others as pastors and teachers, to equip the holy ones for the work of ministry, for building up the body of Christ, until we all attain to the unity of faith and knowledge of the Son of God...so that we may no longer be infants, tossed by waves and swept along by every wind of teaching arising from human trickery..." Scripture writers alone are not enough "for building up the body of Christ..."

Rom. 10:17 – "Thus faith comes from what is heard, and what is heard comes through the word of Christ." St. Paul upholds oral instruction and tradition. Indeed, nowhere in the Bible do we see a single conversion that stems from someone just reading the scriptures.

Ex. 28:30 – The oracle of God is spoken through high priest via the Urim and the Thummim. These mysterious oracular devices were in no way scriptural. Yet the scriptures tell us that in ancient times, the Israelites consulted them regularly to determine the will of God. Thus, the Jewish people were not proponents of the doctrine of "sola scriptura."

Deut. 17:8-12 – The Old Testament had its own form of the Magisterium, one in which disagreements were to be settled by priests and judges: "Any man who has the insolence to refuse to listen to the priest...shall die." The high priests spoke with the authority of God. This passage alone is a refutation of "sola scriptura." Nowhere in the scriptures do we see "scripture alone" upheld as the final authority of our faith.

2 Tim. 3:14 – "...You remain faithful to what you have learned and believed, because you know from whom you learned it..." In other words, spiritual authority is derived from apostolic succession, not "scripture alone." Yet "sola scriptura" would have us hold that the words of apostles who did not write—Andrew, Thaddeus, Bartholomew and the rest—had little or no authority, since their writings were not recorded in the scriptures. St. Paul's statement here indicates quite clearly that the Church's authority, at its most fundamental level, derives from apostleship, not from the scriptures.

1 Cor. 15:11 – Again St. Paul upholds the oral tradition: "...so we preach and so you believed." Nowhere in scriptures do we see a single individual who is converted by "scripture alone." And St. Paul never states, "...so we *write* and so you believed."

Acts 2:42 – St. Luke upholds oral teaching: "They devoted themselves to the teaching of the apostles..." As opposed to "the *writings* of the apostles," which St. Luke of course never states.

Mt. 2:23 – Oral tradition is cited as authoritative: "...so that what had been spoken through the prophets might be fulfilled." Note that not all the prophets wrote. Yet "sola scriptura" would have us believe that their words had no authority until they were written down into the sacred texts. Nathan never wrote a single word that we know of. So when he spoke, were his words not deemed authoritative? When he intoned to David, "Thou art the man," were his words not divinely inspired? Clearly David felt they were, and he treated them as pronouncements from the mouth of God.

Mt. 10:19-20 – Jesus testifies to the fact that the Holy Spirit inspires more than just the scriptures. He can also inspire our speech: "'When they hand you over, do not worry about how you are to speak or what you are to say. You will be given at that moment what you are to say. For it will not be you who speak but the Spirit of your Father speaking through you.'"

Jn. 21:25 – Not everything Christ did and said is in scripture: "There are also many other things that Jesus did, but if these were to be described individually, I do not think the whole world would contain the books that would be written." Are these things not worthy of our consideration because they were not written down? Would the apostles have failed to discuss these things because they somehow foresaw that they would not be written down? The absurdity of such a notion is obvious—but "sola scriptura" requires one to hold some such position, because it denies authority to the words of Jesus that did not happen to have been recorded on paper.

Is. 59:21 – Inspired oral tradition passes from generation to generation: "...my words that I have put into your mouth shall never leave your mouth, nor the mouths of your children." Note that the prophet refers here to the spoken word. This is a clear reference to the Sacred Tradition that is preserved and passed on from one generation to the next. Note as well the involvement of the Holy Spirit, by whom the prophet's speech is inspired. It seems that it is not the "scripture alone" which is God-breathed.

1 Cor. 14:3 – Not all of God's truth is imparted through scripture. St. Paul says the prophets also are prompted by the Holy Spirit for the benefit of the faithful: "...one who prophesies does speak to human beings, for their building up, encouragement, and solace."

2 Pet. 3:1-2 – "...I am trying to stir up your sincere disposition, to recall the words previously spoken by the holy prophets and the commandment of the Lord and Savior through your apostles." The key word is "spoken," not "written."

2 Chron. 19:6-10 – When God instructs the priests on how to settle disputes, he does not instruct them to go to the scriptures to arrive at their decisions: "...and he said to them: 'Take care what you do, for you are judging, not on behalf of man, but on behalf of the Lord; he judges with you. And now, let the fear of the Lord be upon you. Act carefully, for with the Lord, our God, there is no injustice, no partiality, no bribe-taking.'"

Mal. 2:7 – "...The lips of the priest are to keep knowledge, and instruction is to be sought from his mouth, because he is the messenger of the Lord of hosts." The priest has the authority to instruct, not just to read from scripture.

Rom. 6:16-17 – "...You have become obedient from the heart to the pattern of teaching to which you were entrusted." Paul is explicit. Our obedience is to apostolic teaching, not to scripture. Indeed, scripture was never intended to teach the faith at all, but only to strengthen the believers in their faith. In the Bible, we see individuals being instructed by teaching and preaching – never, not even a single time, by "scripture alone."

Gen. 17:14 – "If a male is uncircumcised, that is, if the flesh of his foreskin has not been cut away, such a one shall be cut off from his people; he has broken my covenant." The apostles were not adhering to the authority of the "scripture alone" when they countermanded this clear and ancient teaching and declared that Gentile converts did not need to be circumcised. The apostles felt they had the authority to receive inspiration in addition to the scriptures—specifically, the Holy Spirit's guidance of Sts. Peter and Paul to accept uncircumcised Gentiles into the Church—which cast the scriptures in a totally new and unexpected light. But any Jewish adherent of "sola scriptura" at that time would have been altogether scandalized, incensed—and wrong.

Jer. 23:1-4 – "I myself will gather the remnant of my flock from all the lands to which I have driven them and bring them back to their meadow; there they shall increase and multiply. I will appoint shepherds for them who will shepherd them so that they need no longer fear and tremble; and none shall be missing, says the Lord." Nowhere does God say he will protect his sheep by providing for them the scriptures. Instead, he raises up leaders from the community for them to follow, shepherds through whom he guides them. He is still doing so.

The canon of the scriptures was established by Pope St. Damasus I around the year 400 A.D. Prior to that, there was no agreement in the early Church on which of the hundreds of texts which were believed by some to be sacred were actually inspired. So for nearly 400 years—a time roughly equivalent to the period from the establishment of the first permanent American settlement at Jamestown till today—there was no Bible for a Christian to refer to. Everyone who learned the faith was taught it by another—the same method of instruction used by the apostles. Eventually, the Church in her authority, under the inspiration of the Holy Spirit, determined the canon of the scriptures, which provided the faithful with a reliable reference for use in the building up of the faith. So if we believe the scriptures are truly inspired, then it follows that the Church must be infallible, for it was the Church's authority—not the scriptures themselves—that declared these specific writings to be God-breathed. And if the Church is not infallible in her teachings, then we cannot assume the scriptures she validated are God-breathed, since the authority that declared them so is not trustworthy. So if the Catholic Church can err, then we must condemn the scriptures she has passed down to us as spurious. Trusting the Bible while distrusting the Church that assembled, pronounced, and then protected the Bible through the ages flies in the face of both logic and history. Without the Catholic Church, the Bible would never have been.

THE "RAPTURE"

Many Fundamentalist and Evangelical Protestants adhere to a belief known as the "Rapture." There are many variations on the "Rapture" doctrine. The popular "Left Behind" series of novels, written by Lahaye and Jenkins, presents just one of them. To defend their ideas, Rapturists cite a few broad-brushed passages of scripture, including 1 Thess. 4:15-17 ("…we who are alive, who are left until the coming of the Lord, will surely not precede those who have fallen asleep. For the Lord himself, with a word of command, with the voice of an archangel and with the trumpet of God, will come down from heaven, and the dead in Christ will rise first. Then we who are left, will be caught up together with them in the clouds to meet the Lord in the air"), and 1 Cor. 15:51-52 ("We shall not all fall asleep, but we will all be changed, in an instant, in the blink of an eye, at the last trumpet. For the trumpet will sound, the dead will be raised incorruptible, and we shall be changed").

Yet from these few mysterious passages are drawn precise and detailed predictions that fill volumes, complete with timetables, dates, charts and graphs. The version propounded in the "Left Behind" books is known as pre-millennial, pre-tribulational dispensationalism. It states that in the future the earth will experience a literal 1,000-year reign of Jesus. Just prior to this reign, "true believers" will be "raptured" by Jesus and lifted up by him, secretly and silently, into the clouds. (Never mind that the Bible mentions a loud voice and a trumpet; most Rapturist claim the event will take place in secrecy.) Those unfortunate ones who are "left behind" will suffer a seven-year period of tribulations—a sort of last chance for faith. At the conclusion of the seven years, Jesus will return—for a second Second Coming—this time, with legions of his faithful ones. Together they will defeat the Antichrist, and the 1,000 year reign of Jesus will ensue on the earth. The irony of all this is that Protestants believe it is the Catholic Church that holds to "unbiblical" teachings, and they cite Catholic doctrines on Mary as the primary example. Yet we find scores of Old and New Testament passages referring to Mary (see the section, "Mary, the Mother of God," in this book), while belief in the "Rapture" is accepted without question—and with very little in the way of scriptural substantiation. It is also ironic that many Protestants believe that the Catholic Church has changed its teachings over the centuries. But the present-day concept of the "Rapture" is found nowhere in Christianity—neither in Protestant nor Catholic literature— until the early nineteenth century, when it was invented by an Anglican priest-turned-fundamentalist-minister named John Nelson Darby.

The Catholic Church's teachings on the end-times are far less detailed—and far less dramatic—than Darby's and Lahaye's. The Church certainly holds to the Second Coming of Jesus (note the line, "He will come again to judge the living and the dead," from the Nicene Creed) and the fact that the faithful will be "caught up" to the Lord at that time, as St. Paul states. However, concerning the date and nature of those events, the Church says little ("But of that day and hour no one knows, not even the angels in heaven, nor the Son, but the Father only" [Mt. 24:36].) For an authoritative look at Catholic teachings concerning the end times, see paragraphs 671-679 in the Catechism of the Catholic Church.

BIBLIOGRAPHY

The following works served as resources for both the scripture references and the ideas represented in this book. Each is excellent in its own way. Tim Staples' tapes, listed first, were particularly instructive. But you will have no trouble finding dozens of books and tapes that will provide you with valuable information in far greater depth and detail than can be presented in this modest volume.

Adam, Karl. *The Spirit of Catholicism.* New York: Crossroad/Herder & Herder, 1997. A remarkable statement on the nature of Catholicism first published in Germany in 1924. One of the most profoundly beautiful books about the faith – and what it means to humanity – ever written. The splendid translation, by Dom Justin McCann, also merits mention.

Currie, David B. *Born Fundamentalist, Born Again Catholic.* San Francisco: Ignatius Press, 1996. A scripture-steeped exploration of one believer's struggle to accept his increasing conviction – prompted by careful study of scripture and history – that the Catholic Church is the one, true, holy and apostolic Church founded by Jesus Christ.

De Sales, St. Francis. *The Catholic Controversy.* Rockford: TAN Books, 1992. A 17th century classic of apologetics written by a great saint to combat error. It resulted in tens of thousands of conversions.

Gibbons, James Cardinal. *Faith of Our Fathers.* Rockford: TAN Books, 1980. A simple, concise, understandable explanation of the Catholic faith by one of the giants of nineteenth century American Catholicism.

Hahn, Scott. *A Father Who Keeps His Promise: God's Covenant Love in Scripture.* Ann Arbor: Servant Publications, 1998. A detailed exploration of the progress of the covenantal relationship between God and man through salvation history, by the man who has been called today's most prominent Bible scholar in America. His courageous conversion – along with those of people like Thomas Howard and Peter Kreeft – initially helped convince many non-Catholic Christians that they should take a closer look at Catholic teachings and their basis in the Bible. Thanks in large part to their love of Christ Jesus and their willingness to suffer for him – and a level of intellectual integrity that would not let them rest until they found the fullness of Truth – the Great Returning has begun.

Hahn, Scott. *The Lamb's Supper: The Mass as Heaven on Earth.* New York: Doubleday, 1999. A captivating picture of the Book of Revelation as a mystical description of the Mass as Jesus' immutable Paschal sacrifice celebrated eternally in Heaven – and constantly on earth.

Hahn, Scott. *Hail, Holy Queen: The Mother of God In the Word of God.* New York: Doubleday, 2001. An engaging exploration of the scriptures that prophesy and reveal the role of Mary in salvation history. As Hahn puts it, to miss Mary is to miss the humanity of our Savior.

Hampsch, John H. C.M.F. *Glad You Asked: Scriptural Answers for our Times.* Huntington, IN: Our Sunday Visitor, 1992. A basic, succinct, scripture-based compendium of Catholic theology and apologetics, written for the layman. Presented in a Q&A format, it discusses cultural as well as doctrinal issues.

Howard, Thomas. *On Being Catholic.* San Francisco: Ignatius Press, 1997. A prominent former Evangelical scholar and author provides a personal witness to the majesty and truth of the Catholic faith. A strikingly beautiful statement of faith, it helps make complex concepts accessible.

Jurgens, William. *The Faith of the Early Fathers.* 3 vols. Collegeville: The Liturgical Press, 1998. An eye-opening digest of the writings of the early Church fathers. Provides clear, unequivocal confirmation that the Catholic Church's doctrines – the priesthood, the sacraments, the primacy of the bishop of Rome, reverence for the Blessed Mother, indeed, virtually everything the Church teaches today – actually date back to the very earliest community of Christian believers; in fact all the way back to the communities of faith who were taught by the apostles themselves. The excellent index allows for quick, illuminating research.

Keating, Karl. *Catholicism & Fundamentalism.* San Francisco: Ignatius Press, 1988. A detailed discussion of the attacks on the Church by fundamentalists.

Key, Paul R. *Ninety-Five Reasons for Becoming or Remaining Catholic.* Steubenville: CHResources, 2000. A personal and insightful account of the thinking of a former Presbyterian minister who, after 18 years of study, realized that, "In the midst of a world which has become very secularized, the Catholic Church has retained a spiritual foundation and spiritual resources that are unmatched among the other churches of the West" (p. 53). Concise, clearly stated, and well organized.

Madrid, Patrick. *Surprised By Truth: Converts Give the Biblical and Historical Reasons for Becoming Catholic.* San Diego: Basilica Press, 1994. Intimate portraits of the sometimes joyful, always anguished journeys of a number of serious, seeking Christians to the Catholic faith.

Madrid, Patrick. *Any Friend of God's Is A Friend of Mine.* San Diego: Basilica Press, 1996. A direct and unembroidered look at the biblical and patristic basis for such critical doctrines as the Communion of Saints, the veneration of Mary and intercessory prayer. An excellent sourcebook for apologists.

Ray, Steven K. *Upon This Rock: St. Peter and the Primary of Rome in Scripture and the Early Church.* San Francisco: Ignatius, 1999. An impressive compendium of texts—from both scripture and the early Church fathers—which establishes beyond question the fact that the entire community of the faithful, from the earliest times, acknowledged Peter's office and authority. Ray's assiduous scholarship has rendered this issue virtually beyond disputing.

Ray, Steven K. *Crossing the Tiber: Evangelicals Discover the Historical Church.* San Francisco: Ignatius Press, 1997. An in-depth account of the conversion of Mr. Ray, a former Baptist and Evangelical, and his family. A detailed chronicle of one man's thought processes, including many allusions to critical scripture passages, as well as the witness of the earliest believers. He covers most of the important issues here – the question of authority, 'scripture alone,' Baptism, the Real Presence, etc.

Rumble, Rev. Dr. Leslie and Carty, Rev. Charles. *Radio Replies.* 3 vols. Rockford: TAN Books, 2001. Fascinating answers to incredibly wide-ranging questions addressed during a long-running radio program dedicated to apologetics.

Shea, Mark P. *By What Authority?: An Evangelical Discovers Catholic Tradition.* Huntington, IN: Our Sunday Visitor, 1996. A clear and powerful look at the arguments for and against "sola scriptura" and Church authority. Rich in both scripture and history, it presents a compelling, clear, and rational case.

Staples, Tim. *Biblical Apologetics Course, All Generations Shall Call Me Blessed.* Orange, CA: St. Joseph Communications. Mr. Staples, now a celebrated Catholic apologist, is a former evangelical whose intellectual integrity and hunger for the truth drew him—despite some "kicking and screaming"—to embrace the Catholic faith. In the tapes he provides stirring, scripture-based explanations of the Church's teachings in a variety of areas.

Sungenis, Robert A. *Not By Scripture Alone.* Santa Barbara: Queenship, 1998. An exhaustive, enlightening – and, to my mind anyway, decisive – exploration of this key issue between Catholic and Protestant believers.

Biblical Evidence For Catholicism website, by Dave Armstrong. An excellent source for a tremendous variety of information on the Catholic faith, including references to scriptures, Catholic thinkers, Church history, hyperlinks to other Catholic sites, and dialogues and debates about the faith. At this printing, the URL for the site remains:

http://ic.net/~erasmus/erasmus.htm

Whatever is of merit in this small work is due to the scholarship and insights of the authors whose works are listed here, and of untold other believers who have shared their wisdom throughout the ages. And of course whatever is lacking or incorrect in this book is due to the compiler's innumerable faults, failings, and limitations. If any teaching, thought, sentence, or word of this book contradicts the teaching of the Catholic Church, it is only through ignorance. As always, when in doubt, cling to the Rock, the successor to St. Peter, and the Catholic Church, which Jesus placed in his care.

ACKNOWLEDGEMENTS

Thanks to Carl Olson, Brent Arias, Fr. Fred Barr, Martin Beckman, Jamie Gilcrest, Dave Keene, Joselyn Schutz, Dave Turner, John Hellman, John-Paul Ignatius, Andrew Holt, Tony Kovach, Patrick Sweeney, Patrick Madrid, Jay Damien, Dave Armstrong, Mario Derkson, Larry Nolte and the rest of the cinapol contributors, 1998 and 1999, for their wisdom and their perspicacity. Particular thanks to Robert Sungenis for his fascinating insight into the 1 Samuel passage in the section on "Free Will," and to the distinguished Mr. Olson for lighting the way through the thickets of speculation and fear that enmesh the Protestant doctrine of the "Rapture."

Thanks are also due *This Rock* and *Envoy*, two excellent and useful magazines of the Catholic faith. For subscription information in the U.S., dial 1-888-291-8000 (for 'This Rock') and 1-800-55-ENVOY (for 'Envoy').

And heartfelt thanks to the various Protestant believers with whom I have been privileged to share fellowship and faith, particularly Pastor Paul L., Michael, Sharon S., Mike R., Liz M., Hal F., Bob B., Tim C. and Vance S. Their many hours of inquiries, assertions and disputations prompted research into many of the matters contained here.

Thanks too to my friend and brother in Christ, Van, whose questions and wanderings among so many faith traditions led to much research and many discussions, and finally to his incorporation into the Mystical Body of Christ. Truly, "…all things work for good for those who love God…"

Also, many thanks to Mark B., Joe M., Joe Z., Joe K., Michael B., Steve A. and Jason W., who kindly assisted in the production of the original booklets. And to Fr. McCloskey, Stephen Ray and Dr. Hahn for their gracious encouragement, which was very much appreciated.

I am greatly indebted to many true and generous friends, especially to Jay Damien, whose dedication and enthusiasm – very much in the spirit of St. Francis – opened so many doors and revived the project when it needed reviving.

And I will always be grateful to the scores of steadfast, faith-filled, relentlessly energetic partners who have graced this project over the years. They assisted in every possible way; sacrificing time, effort, money, energy; risking embarrassment; sharing their passion for Christ Jesus and the Church he gave to all humanity; sharing faith; suggesting passages; radiating confidence, and always exhibiting a willingness to do whatever was required. Without these good, full-hearted people – and groups – this project would have sputtered and died years ago. Naturally, I know – dilatory record-keeper that I am – that I am leaving many of you out. I ask your pardon. For, truly, I remain sincerely and eternally grateful to each one of you, and you will always remain in my prayers:

Jamie G., Cynthia O., Paul and Carol D., Paul P., Carolyn S., Jeff L., Jackie Z., Peg S., Michael B., Rose Mary D., Frank W., Lee Anne M., Val G., Kimberly M., Anne A., Joel B., Charlotte M., Marion L., Mary Ann W., Sr. Padre Pio, Rick O., Julie H., Marlena L., Kent M., Chris L., Sharon C., Lori L., Michael and Melanie S., Dottie N., Madeline N., Edward L., Glenn S., Davin W., Kay S., Sue T., Peter S., Julie W., Tim O., Kim P., Patty B., Skip and Georgie N., Bernadette K., Glenn F., Earl M., Connie G., Macile, Stephen P., Maureen G., Judy B., Sandy S., Karl M., Judy L., Mark and Ann L., Larry L., Pat D., Kathi H., Andrea M., Lori L., April L., Marco C., Elizabeth S., Ty A., Richard H., Greg M., The Catholic Information Center, The Catholic Shop Online, Drouillard's Catholic Books, Spread the Word, The Third Order Of St. Francis Arizona, The Coming Home Network, The Good News Shop, Ville De Marie Academy, Bishop Dwenger High School – and so many more – who have helped cast various editions of these little books upon the waters.

And thanks to Shala Fleece for her excellent and tireless work in helping to sort through years-thick layers of punctuation eccentricities and jury-rigged word-processing formatting to shape this latest edition. I can only hope her soul profited from the penitential suffering.

Thanks, too, to Marcus Grodi and all those who do – or contribute to – the Spirit-brimming work of the estimable Coming Home Network, for seeing to it that this little project continues, and in such unaccustomed style. I am humbled that you have seen fit to include it in your excellent catalogue.

If the reader finds this volume useful, please be kind enough to say a prayer for all the individuals who are credited here, for the firms that publish and distribute the excellent books and tapes cited, and for the faith of the children of the person who compiled this material.

And please, if you are able, be kind enough to remember the Coming Home Network in your charitable giving.

Above all, and for everything always, thanks be to God.

—Gregory Oatis

AUTHOR'S BIOGRAPHY

Gregory Oatis is a lifelong Catholic who rediscovered the mystery and majesty of the Catholic faith late in life. Having learned about the Bible and the Early Church Fathers from the good Sisters of Notre Dame in his Ohio grade school in the late fifties and early sixties, he attended a Jesuit high school in the post-Vatican II era, going on to receive a B.A. in English from the University of Toledo. He began his career in journalism, as a news reporter for the Toledo Blade, and music editor for the Fort Lauderdale Sun-Sentinel. He made the transition to marketing in the early eighties, and has served as creative director and principal in a number of marketing communications agencies in Toledo, Ohio, as well as Marketing Vice President for a world wide equipment supplier. Along the way, he was one of the founders of Blue Suit Records, a recording company specializing in the blues, and co-wrote the book, *Witness to the Blues*, with blues photographer, John Gibbs Rockwood. Mr. Oatis has been active in various parish and diocesan ministries, including RCIA and Stephen Ministry, and has taught the Catholic faith to junior high school students. While still involved with his parish's RCIA program – through which interested individuals are received into the Church – he began researching and recording pertinent Bible passages that affirm the various Catholic teachings disputed by many Protestants. His intention was to provide lists of these verses to those candidates and catechumens whose friends or families were opposed to their conversion. Often, Catholic converts are subjected to attacks from well-meaning Protestants who have little idea of what the Catholic Church actually teaches. Those debates typically range through the pages of scripture – which is only natural, since the Bible is the primary spiritual authority acknowledged by most Protestant denominations. As more people saw the lists, the demand grew – and so did the lists. Eventually, approximately seven thousand copies were distributed through the hard work and charity of dozens of Spirit-filled and generous Catholics. At present, Mr. Oatis is living in Ohio with his wife—whose hard work and faithfulness, he says, are detailed in Proverbs 31—and the youngest of his three bright and talented children. He earns his living providing marketing consultation to a variety of institutions and companies.

For more information
about the author and
The Coming Home Network International,
please write, phone, or visit their website:

The Coming Home Network
PO Box 8290
Zanesville, OH 43702-8290

1-800-664-5110

http://www.chnetwork.org

OTHER RESOURCES AVAILABLE
FROM *CHRESOURCES*
AND *THE COMING HOME NETWORK*

How Firm A Foundation
a novel by Marcus Grodi

Stephen LaPointe is a minister who loves Jesus, loves to preach, and considers the Bible as the one sufficient, firm foundation for his life. He left a career to attend seminary because he wanted to devote his life to helping others experience a true conversion of heart. He knows that one day he will stand before God accountable for what he preaches, and it is in this conviction that his crisis begins, for how can he know for certain that what he preaches is eternally true? This crisis threatens his calling as a minister, his marriage, and even his life.

Item # 2582 soft cover- 464 pp. Price $14.95
Item # 4001 12 - 120 min. cassettes Price: $39.95

Ninety-Five Reasons for Becoming or Remaining Catholic
by Paul R. Key

A former Presbyterian pastor shares his ninety-five reasons for becoming and remaining Catholic, including biblical, historical, practical, spiritual, and Eucharistic reasons. A few specifics: 1) Scripture teaches the real presence, not just symbolism. 2) Sola scriptura is unbiblical.

Item # 2521 soft cover - 103 pages Price: $9.00

Roots of the Reformation

by Karl Adams

Most Protestants understand the Reformation from only one perspective. As a Catholic, Karl Adams gives a historically sensitive and accurate analysis of the causes of the Reformation that stands as a valid and sometimes unsettling challenge to the presuppositions of Protestants and Catholics alike. *Roots of the Reformation* is a powerful summary of the issues that led to the reformation and their implications today.

Item # 2523 soft cover - 108 pp. Price: $5.00

Catechism Tabs

Tabs for the updated *Catechism of the Catholic Church - 2ⁿᵈ edition* give quick and easy reference of the teachings of the Church on 25 topics and include a subject index. Easily find any topic.

Item # 2597   **Price: $4.00**

Daily Scripture & Catechism Devotional Reading Guide

By making a commitment of only twenty to thirty minutes a day, you can prayerfully read through the entire Bible and/or Catechism in one year! Take whatever Bible translation you like that contains the entire Canon of Scripture, your Catechism, and start reading! This is especially a great tool for Bible study groups.

Item # 3010   **Price: $.50**